ADVANCE PRAISE

"Halina Kleiner, at age 91, finally put on paper, with the help of her co-author, Edwin Stepp, the true story of her life as a child survivor of the Holocaust. Her book *My March Through Hell* recounts Kleiner's six-year journey from young, innocent teenager to experienced and savvy survivor of German torture and a witness to mass murder. This book is especially valuable in its tale of Halina's experiences on one of the notorious German "Death Marches," when towards the end of the war, Jews who had survived the starvation and brutality of German concentration and labor camps were placed on forced marches out of the camps to prevent Allied soldiers from finding these emaciated witnesses to the mass murders committed by the Nazis. This book is outstanding and unusual in its many emotionally stirring details of Halina's brutal death march, which resulted in the deaths of so many of those prisoners forced on the "march." Halina credits her survival at each step of her incarceration by the Nazis to luck. But luck, coincidence, happenstance are all a sideshow in this inspirational book. Halina is much too modest and fails to credit her amazing bravery, derring-do, intelligence and cleverness that are largely the real reasons she survived terror and trauma. She made decisions when or how to run away or to stay put, whom to trust and whom to not trust. Whether it was a sixth sense or something else, Halina used judgment, guile and her intelligence to enable her to escape—for a time—capture by the Nazis or their collaborators during and immediately after the war. It is true, as Halina points out, that many victims of the Nazi terror survived years of terror and torture through cleverness until their "luck" finally "ran out." But it is impossible to read Halina's story without feeling tremendous admiration for this 13-18 year old girl, wise beyond her years who outsmarted the Nazis and foiled their plans to murder her. An equally important theme of this book is that relationships among the prisoners played a large role in their survival. Those who lived alone, died alone. Halina established a close relationship with two other young girls who helped each other in countless ways in the camp and literally supporting the one who could no longer walk on their Death March—continuously encouraging each other to keep hope alive. This book is destined to become a classic and a must read in junior high school and above grades. It teaches the history of the terrible things the Nazis inflicted on their Jewish victims without terrifying nor overwhelming junior high or high school readers. It will encourage young readers who will empathize with Halina to think about what they would do in desperate situations. It will inspire readers to appreciate their own lives and to accept or improve their lives without losing hope if they find themselves in difficult situations. In many ways, this book is far better to assign to junior high and high school readers than *The Diary of Anne Frank*. Read this and you'll understand."

- **Kenneth P. Price, PhD.** *Author of Separated Together. The Incredible True WWII Story of Soulmates Stranded an Ocean Apart*

"Halina Kleiner and I endured the Volary Death March together. She was five years younger than me, and because of that I was amazed at her strength and resilience during those horrible months. I am so glad she finally is telling her story. It is a gripping tale of her many narrow escapes and a symbol of endurance and courage in the face of unspeakable evil."

- **Gerda Weissmann Klein (1924-2022),** Polish-American award-winning writer and human rights activist. Author of *All but My Life* (1957), a memoir about her experiences during the Holocaust. She was a recipient of the Presidential Medal of Freedom from Barack Obama in 2011.

MY MARCH THROUGH HELL

A YOUNG GIRL'S TERRIFYING JOURNEY TO SURVIVAL

HALINA KLEINER
EDWIN STEPP

ISBN 9789493276307 (ebook)

ISBN 9789493276284 (paperback)

ISBN 9789493276291 (hardcover)

Publisher: Amsterdam Publishers, The Netherlands

info@amsterdampublishers.com

My March Through Hell is part of the series Holocaust Survivor Memoirs World War II

Halina's husband Leon Kleiner also published his memoirs *Save My Children* in this series

Copyright © Halina Kleiner, 2022

Cover image: Photo of the Volary Death March, Oberhaid, Czech Lands, 4 May 1945.

All Rights Reserved. No part of this publication may be reproduced or transmitted in any form or by any means, electronic or mechanical, including photocopy, recording or any other information storage and retrieval system, without prior permission in writing from the publisher.

CONTENTS

Introduction	ix
Just Before the War: The Last Holiday	1
The War Begins: From the Frying Pan to the Fire	5
Early in the War: Escape Back Home	11
Caught Without an Armband	14
Into the Ghetto	17
Aktion! Death Comes to Czestochowa	23
Ransacked!	29
On the Edge of the Ghetto	32
Ms. Sporna	36
"You Cannot Stay"	39
Alone on the Run	43
Hiding in the Attic	46
Die Alone or Die With My People?	52
Seeing Father One Last Time	56
Arranging A Dangerous Escape Plan	60
Smuggled to Bedzin	66
Reunited with My Grandparents	72
Into the Camps-Bolkenhain	77
On to Landeshut	82
Moved Again-Grünberg Camp	86
The SS Take Over	90
The March Begins	94
Into the Cold-From Grünberg to Bautzen	100
The Execution at Bautzen	104
On A Bridge in Dresden	109
Helmbrecht's Hell	113
Back on the March-Neuhausen	119
Onto Czechoslovakia with No Food	123
A Defiant Greeting from the Czechs	129
Goodbye, Dear Halinka	133
Escape at Last!	138

The German Farmer	143
The War is Over	147
Hospital in Prachatice	151
Nursing Back to Health	155
Returning to Human	159
On to Austria	162
Displaced with Lonek-Salzburg	166
Leaving Salzburg	170
Reunited	174
To America	178
Buffalo and Gerda	181
Surviving America	186
Looking Back	190
Afterword	195
Acknowledgments	199
Photos	201
About the Authors	209
Amsterdam Publishers Holocaust Library	213

INTRODUCTION

Why write this book? Does history need another Holocaust story? With the hundreds of thousands already written and recorded, does one more make any difference in establishing the truth of that horrible event? Will another gruesome and horrifying account help prevent it from happening again?

It is stupefying to me that there are still people who deny the Holocaust. Adding my tale to the mountains of evidence already accumulated will not change those minds. It is one thing to deny it and quite another to spread the lie that it did not happen. Those that engage in the latter need to be countered continually and loudly with every existing story that has been told and those that have yet to be told. As we get further and further away from the Second World War, succeeding generations need to have every one of these accounts available for review and testimony.

My generation and those of my people who survived the Holocaust constantly repeat "Never Forget!" The horror of that time is still fresh in our memories. For those who did not live through it and those who will come after us, the only way they can "Never Forget" is to have our memories become theirs. And the way to do that is by recording every single story that can be recorded.

That is why I finally felt I needed to write this book.

I also often think about those who never got a chance to tell their stories. It is estimated that two out of three Jews living in Europe before the war lost their lives. Some of those who died did have their stories told by others after the war. For most of them, we will never know what happened.

Therefore, I write this book also for them. The reason I survived and the others did not was sheer luck. It was not because I was smarter or stronger or more wily. I just happened to be in the right places at the right times to escape death. My story is one long string of narrow escape after narrow escape; fortunate circumstance after fortunate circumstance; lucky break after lucky break. Six million of my people saw their luck run out eventually. They cannot tell their stories. I am still able to tell mine. So I feel I have an obligation to them to put my story in writing in the most detailed way.

I have told my story in 1987, when I was interviewed at Kean University in Union, New Jersey. The four hours of video is available online, but that was not the full account. Due to time constraints we were unable to record quite a few parts of it. It took me many years to finally tell the fuller version. At 91 years old, I know there is probably not much more time for me to do that. So my resolve was strengthened to get it done.

My delay in doing so was not because, like so many Holocaust survivors, I could not bear to revisit the horrible events. On the contrary, I talked often about them with my friends who also were survivors. I often recounted the story to my family, my children, and especially to my husband Leon. His story of survival is also remarkable and unique, and he published it as, *Save My Children. The Astonishing Tale of Survival and its Unlikely Hero*

(Amsterdam Publishers, 2020). His ability to complete the difficult task inspired me to follow his example.

Had I taken up the pen earlier in my life, it would have been easier for me to complete. But life was too busy, and I could not find the time among my other, perhaps more important, family duties. The most difficult time in my life was during the war, of course. Yet, life after that in America was no bowl of cherries. We worked hard to build a successful business and raise three beautiful children, one of whom we lost to cancer. My son David died of brain cancer at an all too young age and that tragedy has haunted us throughout our lives. I write this book with him in mind. He was also not able to write or tell his story, although, had he survived, I know it would have been a bright one.

JUST BEFORE THE WAR: THE LAST HOLIDAY
AUGUST 1939

The hot summer day was coming to a close. Sadness was starting to overtake me as I knew our holiday had reached its last day. I sat outside our hotel room and thought about the gorgeous mountains all around me and what a fabulous time the past few weeks had been with my mother and my grandmother. Even though I wished we could stay longer, I was missing my father, and knowing we would see him again soon, cheered me a bit.

The resort towns of the Caucasus Mountains were a favorite of Europeans from everywhere. The beautiful countryside, cascading rivers, sparkling lakes, and hiking trails that covered the landscape were a wonderful escape from the demands and pressures of the bustling cities of Poland, Austria, Ukraine, and Czechoslovakia. Perhaps it was the plentiful hot springs that inspired millions of Eastern Europeans to make the area their holiday destination every year. The region was noted for its many luxurious and not-so-luxurious spas featuring these healing waters.

My family was among those tourists every year. We stayed at some lovely places, but they were more of the "not-so-luxurious" resorts that we could afford. As a young preteen girl, I did not know the difference. We could have slept in tents, and I would have loved the experience just the same. The excitement that welled up inside me as August approached could not be contained. And when the time would come to board the train for the long journey southward, it was like releasing the lid on a pressure cooker. Finally, we were off to paradise.

We typically would spend several weeks at the resort. We had all kinds of exciting and relaxing activities in which to participate: hiking the steep slopes, swimming in the lakes and rivers, and sometimes just sitting around doing nothing. I loved to read, so the latter was not at all boring to me.

I loved reading so much, that often my only birthday and Chanukah presents were books. There was nothing that I could receive that would have made me happier.

On that late August day in 1939, we were finishing up the packing for our train trip home. As we closed the last bags, I heard my mother and grandmother talking in nervous and frightened tones. There was a sense of great urgency in their voices. We should hurry as fast as possible to the station. They had heard bad news about the political tensions engulfing the continent.

Hitler and Stalin had just signed their infamous pact of nonaggression. It would only be days before the Nazi dictator would invade Poland setting off the Second World War. As a ten-year-old, I did not know much about international politics, but I was aware of the threat of war. The menacing German nation had been rattling its sabers for a long time. I understood enough even at my young age about the dangers that had been looming to share my mother's and grandmother's fears.

As we approached the small train station, we could see a flurry of activity. Normally this station was uncrowded and quiet. But now there were more people than usual and there was a sense of anxiety in their movements. Our horse and buggy arrived outside with a few others at the same time. People on foot rushed toward the station doorway dragging their suitcases. Little children scurried frantically behind parents trying to keep up.

Our buggy arrived and we threw open the doors and jumped out. A nearby conversation between two men revealed to us the news. Tensions were increasingly rapidly between Germany and Poland and the threat of war was growing. These tourists realized it may be impossible to get back home if they did not leave soon.

We rushed into the rail terminal to find the anxiety even greater inside. People pressed and pushed each other in the unruly cues leading to the ticket windows. Fortunately, we already had our tickets for the return journey. Our train would be leaving soon.

We wasted no time and headed for the track. We were relieved to see the train was there and was steaming and rumbling as it warmed up for its departure. Passengers ran for the gangways and threw their luggage up and into the doors. The conductors waved their arms to hurry them onto the train. We found our car and moved as quickly as we could to our seats. I plopped down in my seat next to the window and relaxed. I was eager to see my father again and ready for the soothing rhythm of the train to rock me to sleep.

The rail car lurched forward and the metal of its wheels and hitches screeched. It was moving, but only for a second and then it stopped again. Another lurch and this time the movement continued. Very slowly, the train inched away from the terminal. Its speed built and with every increase, my heartbeat slowed from its frightened pace all the excitement had caused. We were on our way home. My mother and my grandmother breathed big sighs of relief. The tension left my body and I settled back into my seat, ready to close my eyes and sleep.

Later, we learned that our train was the last to leave the station that day. A stroke of luck. I had no idea at that moment how many other strokes of luck I was going to need and experience in the next six years.

THE WAR BEGINS: FROM THE FRYING PAN TO THE FIRE
SEPTEMBER 1939

When we arrived in our hometown of Częstochowa, the mood was grim. Everyone expected the worst, not only the Jews, but also the Poles. On August 31, the day we arrived back home, SS agents, disguised as Polish soldiers, carried out several false flag raids on German buildings and installations on the Polish-German border. These would be used to justify the invasion of Poland. The next day, September 1, 1939, the dreaded news came. The German army swiftly moved across the border and the German air force began bombing Warsaw.

Częstochowa was right on the German border. Because of that, many people in the city expected to be right in the midst of heavy fighting. My father did not want my mother and me to be at risk of the bombing and gun fire. He decided that the best thing would be to send us to our relatives who lived much further from the border. The town was called Skierniewice and was on the outskirts of Warsaw.

My father wasted no time. He had us pack up our clothes and other necessary belongings. Then he called a taxi. He could not get a train for us and the other method of transportation in those days, horse and buggy, would be slower and riskier. My father decided to pay the hefty fare for a taxi to take us all the way to Skierniewice, which was over 150 kilometers away.

We did not know how long we would be gone, so we took more things with us than we eventually needed. We filled sacks not only with clothes, but also with bedding and pillows. When the taxi arrived, it was clear that there would not be room enough for all our belongings as well as my mother and me. So my father helped the driver remove the back seat. We piled our sacks into the back where the seat had been, and I climbed in on top of them. My mother sat in front with the driver. What a spectacle we must have been for anyone who saw us pass.

The relatives we were going to stay with were on my mother's side of the family. I don't remember their exact relationship to us. They were not originally from this town near Warsaw. My mother and her family were from Silesia, which is a region in southern Poland along the borders of the Czech Republic and Germany. In fact, the region of Silesia spreads across those three countries. Most of it was in Poland. She was from the town of Będzin, one of a "tri-cities" that are close together—Sosnowiec, Będzin, and Dąbrowa. And like Częstochowa, there was also a very large Jewish community in those towns before the war.

Our relatives greeted us warmly and happily took us in when we arrived. I was thrilled to see my grandmother and grandfather were there. The family had also taken in my aunt and five of my cousins, three girls and two boys. The three girls were unaccompanied by their parents; Their mother had died a year before and their father had stayed behind to protect their home just as my father had done. The two boys, Jurek and Nusiek, were there with my aunt Saba. My three girl cousins were Mila, Fela, and Gucia, all much younger than me, and I helped take care of them all.

That experience made me wonder what it would have been like to have younger siblings. I was an only child, but I came close to having a sister or a brother. My mother became pregnant earlier that year and would suffer a miscarriage sometime in the spring. I grieved for my mother but also for myself since I really wanted a sibling. But looking back now, it was probably for the best that we did not have a baby to take care of during the hell that was to come.

It would not be long before we realized the decision to leave Częstochowa was a mistake. The safety we had sought from the German attack would not be found in Skierniewice. The day after we arrived, the fear and terror began. The town was a major railway junction for trains coming in and out of Warsaw and therefore was a primary target for bombing.

When the air raids started, we could hear the planes droning overhead, and in the distance we saw explosions. At first, they were far away but we worried that would not last. The house we were in was close to the railway station. My family lived on the second floor, while a Polish family lived on the first floor. As the bombing increased, we feared that being on the higher floor was riskier. We asked our neighbors if we could wait out the bombing with them. They agreed and we grabbed a few belongings and hurried downstairs.

We all huddled together in one room of the downstairs apartment as the bombs continued to fall nearby. Diligently and fervently, we recited our prayers. Our Christian neighbors were in the next room doing the same. We were saying Shema Yisrael and they were crossing themselves.

Suddenly, a bomb hit very close to the house. It shook the structure violently and the windows shattered. So did our nerves. Plaster from the walls tumbled down all around us. Clouds of dust filled the air. At first, we thought the debris in the air might be poisonous gas. Our relatives remembered how gas had been used in bombings during the First World War. They shouted for us to cover our mouths and noses. We buried our faces in whatever was nearby to keep from inhaling—handkerchiefs, blankets, pillows. I gasped for air through the blanket that covered my mouth. Was it fear or lack of oxygen that suffocated me now? I decided that I should not give into the terror of the moment and try my best to remain calm.

I was terribly frightened and I don't know where the inner strength came from, but I was compelled to do my best to comfort the others in the house, especially my younger cousins who were beginning to cry. I calmly told them that everything was going to be alright, and we would survive. Even the other adults were amazed at my ability to think positively and calmly. It was a good acting job because I was terrified.

Eventually we realized that the dust in the air was not gas and we began to breathe easily again. The bombing continued for a while longer and then subsided a bit. At that point, my family decided it would be better to make our way back to Częstochowa. We knew now that Warsaw would be center of fighting. Even if there was major fighting in Częstochowa, we felt it would be better to be together as a family. We realized it would be very risky to be on the move at this moment, yet we felt that it could not be any worse than staying in the middle of the heavy fighting.

My mother and I packed up our things, while my grandfather left to find some method of transportation. Soon, he returned and told us that he had hired a horse-drawn wagon that was big enough to carry us all. After a little while the wagon came, and we all piled into it. Slowly, we made our way out to the main road leading westward toward Częstochowa. As the wagon turned onto the road, it became clear that it would not be easy to get out of the city. The road was clogged with people trying to flee. We moved along at a snail's pace but, at least for now, we were moving.

We turned a corner, and the traffic jam was met by Polish soldiers marching in the opposite direction. We were forced off the road to make room for them. German airplanes screamed noisily overhead, while the bombings continued. We realized that the wagon was going to be no use. Staying in it made us sitting ducks for the air raids. Suddenly, a fighter plane appeared in the sky just ahead of us. It flew straight toward the Polish troops and then dipped down. The popping of machine gun bullets sent the soldiers diving into the ditches. We hid under the wagon and waited for the strafing to stop. Now we knew for certain we should continue the journey on foot.

We made our way to some nearby woods and continued westward. At the end of the day, we came to a shtetl called Biala. We decided to stay here for the night and try to continue in the morning. The next day, German troops arrived in the little village. We were very frightened, but felt being here would be better than meeting the army alone on the road. At least here we were with other Jews and perhaps would not be singled out.

The troops arrived in Biala without any fight from the Poles. The only real Polish resistance was taking place in Warsaw at the time. Quickly the Germans established control of the Biala. They commanded all the Jews come to the marketplace. I remember going there and seeing all the people gathered there. This shtetl was populated entirely by Jews. Hundreds of them waited for instructions.

Fortunately, there was no attempt to capture or kill any of us like the Germans were doing in other Polish towns when they first invaded. In some Jewish shtetls, Jews were forced to the main squares of their towns and shot on the spot. Just a few days after invading my hometown of Czestochowa, Wermacht soldiers murdered about 150 Jews as well as hundreds of Poles. This came to be known as "Bloody Monday" in the history of the town.

Of course, we had no knowledge of the incident, having left before the Germans arrived. So, as we stood in the square of Biala, we had no idea what to expect. My memory is not good enough to remember what we were told. I am quite certain we were commanded to stay there and not leave the shtetl. We were not imprisoned or even forced into a ghetto at that point. But the Germans maintained strict control and, as a result, my family could not leave Biala for many weeks.

EARLY IN THE WAR: ESCAPE BACK HOME
OCTOBER 1939

While in Biala, things continued to get worse. There was still no move to kill Jews here, but we struggled to find food and other necessities. I worried about my father. Was he OK? Had he been captured and sent away to a labor camp? Was he even still alive? I wanted so desperately to know and to see him again.

Six weeks had passed, and we were still under orders to stay put in this village. We were growing restless and anxious of what might come if we continued to stay there. I was desperate to get back to Częstochowa and my impatience was growing stronger every day. I began to push my mother to leave. She was also eager but was still afraid of the danger. Regardless, I kept pestering her, pleading to go home and see my father.

Finally, my mother agreed that we should take the chance to return. While things for Jews all over Poland deteriorated, life for the Poles slowly returned to some normality. Train travel was once again frequent and possible. And freight trains were running even more frequently. For Jews, getting a ticket for a passenger train was impossible. We had heard that people were able to hop on freight trains and, while risky, the Germans were preoccupied with other things to police this completely. We decided to take the risk and find a train back to our hometown.

We said goodbye to my grandparents, aunts, and cousins. They were also making their own plans to get back to their homes in Silesia. It was an emotional scene knowing we might not ever see each other again. We were afraid for them and for ourselves. Tearfully, we began the walk to the nearby train station.

Biala did not have a train station, so we had to walk to another nearby town. Fortunately, on this day there were no police or soldiers in sight. Even so, we were careful to remain as inconspicuous as possible. I wanted to run to the station because I was so eager to get back home, but we tried to walk without any sign of nervousness or panic.

After some time, we arrived at the station which was not large, but busy. We were not the only people trying to leave. Carefully we surveyed the area and continued our effort to blend in. Most passenger trains did not stop here since it was such a small village. They only slowed as they moved past the platform where we stood to return to full speed once they had passed. Freight trains were not scheduled to stop here either, but occasionally they would come to a halt in the station yard as they waited for other trains to clear further down the lines.

I do not know how my mother determined which train was going in the right direction. But she found a train with a mail car that was headed toward Częstochowa. We scurried up the ladder and into it. There were a few other refugees sitting on the floor of the car. Perhaps one of them had told my mother where it was bound.

The journey on the train was not a long way, but the train often stopped. Before the day was over, we were back in Częstochowa. When we finally arrived, my heart leaped. It was filled with excitement that I might soon see my father again. It was also filled with dread, not knowing if he would still be there. For almost two months, we had not heard anything from him. What would we find?

Once off the train, we made our way quickly back to our neighborhood and our apartment. As we turned the final corner and started down our street, my anxiety became almost unbearable. I quickened my pace and was leaving my mother many yards behind. Soon I was at our front door. I pounded on it a couple of times before flinging it open. I bounded inside and called out for my father. In a flash he was in front of me, and we grabbed each other tightly. Tears streamed down my face. My mother caught up to me and joined us in our hug. I let go and let the two of them enjoy a hug alone.

I remembered the joy and hugs we shared when we returned from our long summer vacations. Those were so sweet and memorable. Remembering this now is bittersweet. It would be the last time the three of us would have such an emotional reunion.

CAUGHT WITHOUT AN ARMBAND
OCTOBER 1939

What a relief to be back home and reunited with my father. We had escaped the horror of the bombing around Warsaw and the anxiety of waiting six weeks for the right time to leave Biala. Things were dramatically different now. My father's business had been taken from him. German soldiers commandeered rooms in our house to live and work in. They kept to themselves, and we were more than happy to do the same. It was very tense, but at least for now, we were not under any threat of being killed.

My father had become a different man. His business had been stolen, his very livelihood and source of confidence taken. He was devastated. No longer did I see the strong and decisive man that he had been as I grew up. He was fearful, and anxiety plagued him. He worried out loud about what our fate might be. Often, he was too afraid to leave the house. My mother and I took care of the essential duties that required going out in the town.

There were shortages of everything we needed, including food and clothing. Finding them took great courage, ingenuity, and effort. I had to become resourceful. I did my best to encourage my father as often as I could. I don't know where this resolve came from, but I felt I should remain positive and optimistic to help relieve his anxiety. Looking back, this probably prepared me for what was to come over the next few years.

Immediately after the war began, Jewish children were prohibited to go to school. I loved school and worried about being away from it for too long. Despite the ban, one of my former teachers organized some classes for the Jewish children in the area. This instruction was done in secret and with great risk. Had we been caught, it could have meant being sent off to a concentration camp or, worse, death. Somehow, we managed to make it happen and were never discovered.

Very early after the Germans arrived, we were forced to wear armbands identifying us as Jews. These armbands with the Star of David sewn onto them are perhaps the most remembered image from the Holocaust, so requires no description. At first, young children under the age of ten did not need to wear them. Although I was ten years old when the war started, I did not wear one for a while. I don't remember if we just didn't know the exact age or if my parents thought I looked young enough to get away with it. Whatever the reason, it put me in a dangerous situation.

One Saturday, I left our house to go play with a friend of mine. I was excited to see my friend again and put the worries of the war out of my mind for a the time being. I was dressed nicely and skipped joyfully as I hurried to her house. When I turned a corner, I was suddenly spotted by a member of the infamous "Schupo" police, or *Schutzpolizei*. This branch of state police was brought in from Germany to patrol all over Poland. Those who worked for it had to be a member of the Nazi party and the SS So, you can imagine my fear at encountering him.

He grabbed me by the sleeve and demanded to know why I was not wearing an armband. I told him that I was too young to wear one.

He did not believe me and demanded that I take him back to my house. It wasn't very far, but those few minutes with him had me petrified.

When we arrived, my mother opened the door and almost fainted. The color drained from her cheeks while her face filled with fear. The policeman asked her why I was not wearing an armband. I was so frightened that I don't remember now what she told him. Luckily, he only reprimanded us and let me go. Others who were caught without armbands faced severe punishment and sometimes were immediately sent to concentration camps.

I had escaped a situation that could have cost my parents their lives or my own. From that time on, I never left the house without the armband.

The star as a tactic of identifying Jews was not new to Europe. It had been used at other times over the course of European history. But the Nazis perfected the system and used it as the first step in degrading us. As we passed non-Jews in the streets, they often avoided us and gave us lots of room as they walked by. I never experienced it, but many Jews were simply pushed out of the way or even shoved to the ground as they passed Polish and German people.

For the next year and a half, life remained relatively stable, and our situation did not change much. Life was increasingly difficult, and we lived in constant fear, but we could not imagine the evil that was to come. It was difficult to get information about what was happening in the war. So we tried to believe that things would not get worse. We hoped that the war would somehow come to an end soon. As I remember it, life for us was still bearable considering the circumstances. But in the spring of 1941, that would begin to change rapidly.

INTO THE GHETTO
APRIL 1941

For the first two years of the war, we were allowed to stay in our home. Even though we shared it with German officers and other officials during that time, it gave us a sense of normalcy and comfort to be in a familiar place. It was the only place I had ever lived. It was a nice home. Part of a block of homes in the center of the city, it was relatively large by mid-20th century European standards. And it was comfortable with a large stove heating the house.

For a long time, the Germans had plans to get rid of all Jews. We knew already that things were very bad for Jews all over Poland. We did not know anything yet about the "Final Solution," but we had heard plenty of horrible stories about murders. And we knew about the infamous Warsaw Ghetto and that Jews were being forced into ghettos in other cities around Poland.

In April 1941, it would be our turn to be forced out. When the Częstochowa Ghetto was created, we were quickly uprooted. The part of the city the Germans chose for establishing the ghetto, was the poorest and least desirable area. We were assigned to a small apartment. I often wondered who lived there before. What happened to them and where did they go? Was their fate worse than ours or had they been allowed to go and live in a better place to make room for us. Since they were the poorest of the Poles in town, I doubt it was the latter. Perhaps they were taken away to work in a nearby factory. Or perhaps this apartment had been inhabited by Jews who had already suffered the fate so many more would face.

The new house could barely be called a home; it was dilapidated and dirty. And we were not allowed to bring much from our home. So we would now live an even more meager life, but on the other hand, we did not yet fear for our lives. The threat was always there, of course, but as long as we obeyed the strict rules and did not challenge them, we felt hopeful that we could escape death.

Meanwhile, conditions in this ghetto and the others around Poland quickly deteriorated. People were forced to live together in very crowded conditions. Often more than one family occupied the same house or apartment. The average number of people living in a room in a Polish ghetto seems to have been seven. As a result, it was difficult to keep things clean and sanitary.

That density and lack of hygiene became a disease creator and spreader. Millions of Polish Jews died of typhus and tuberculosis and other communicable diseases because of this confinement. Ghettos were not invented by the Nazis, however. The use of the word "ghetto" for these confinements originated in Venice in 1516 when the rulers of the city forced the Jews living there into one walled section. That area was the former location of a metal foundry. The Italian word for foundry is "ghetto." The Venetian ghetto was not set up to eradicate Jews, but more to isolate them from the Christians in the city. Jews in Venice were allowed to leave during the day to conduct business but had to return at night when the gates to the bridges that led into the section were locked.

The Germans, as they did in so many things, took the idea to a new and frightening level.

At first, the Częstochowa Ghetto was not closed; it did not have walls or barbed wire to separate it from the Polish side. Poles could come and go as they pleased, but Jews were not permitted to leave. Eventually, that would change. Fences were built around it and Poles were forbidden to enter, which created additional hardship for us. When the Poles were allowed in, we could trade for the necessities on the black market that emerged. Once they were forbidden, it became much more difficult to get food and other things we needed. Nothing could come in and nothing could go out.

The Germans provided very little for us in the way of food and other necessities. They slowly tightened their grip and were metaphorically strangling us, but they were about to speed up the process of eliminating us from Europe. Their precise plan for killing us is well documented. They would do it in the most efficient way, slowly and methodical. They gradually took more and more from us and forced us into ever difficult conditions. Like a sadist tightening the screws on a torture device, they enjoyed the long process of seeing us dehumanized. It was an emotional and mental tactic designed to break us. Perhaps had we known what was to come, we may not have been able to endure the mental anguish. Some people sensed that much worse was to come. Many committed suicide rather than waiting for it. Sometimes whole families poisoning themselves. Was that a better fate than allowing the Nazis to have their sadistic pleasures fulfilled?

We did our best to resist this mental torture. Yet, we were fearful that worse was coming. Rumors of the terrible things that were happening in other places reached us; we had learned about the concentration camps. Raids were occurring all over Poland to round up Jews to work in them. And eventually we heard that the purpose of some of these camps was for extermination in which people were being worked to death, or were being gassed.

Now the plan was going to be carried out in Częstochowa. The mass roundup and transport of people started in the summer of 1942. Young men were the first to be targeted in this systematic effort. Sometimes they caught them randomly on the streets. At other times they had lists of names and they came to their houses and arrested them. Or, to our shame, the Jewish officials of the Judenrat were forced to capture them. At this point, they were told it was to go and work in these camps. But we knew the truth.

First, they took our businesses, jobs, and schools away. Then they took us from our homes and put us in the ghetto. Then they divested us of our material possessions. And now they were coming for us.

The ghetto was formed in April 1941. In a little over a year, they came to kill us. On September 22, 1942, the largest aktion began in my hometown. It was the day after Yom Kippur. The Nazis often planned their actions against the Jews on or close to our Holy Days. They reveled in finding ways to add to their cruelty. The evil calculation and use of that tactic is still unfathomable to me.

This aktion would be the beginning of the total liquidation of the city. Like almost every other city in Poland, Jews in Częstochowa had been forced into a ghetto. Once established, over 40,000 were confined to a small area in the poorest part of the city. At its peak, it would bulge with over 48,000 sick and starving inhabitants cramped into tiny and filthy living spaces.

Early in the morning on that day in September, we heard commotion on the streets. German officers and Polish policemen were banging on doors and demanded that everyone came out and should go to the train station. Of course, we were terrified because we knew where the trains leaving with Jews were going—to the extermination camps.

My parents nervously discussed what to do. They quickly derived a plan. My father and I had papers proving that we worked to help the German war effort. He had been working in a local factory and I had worked at a local farm, but my mother did not have any such papers. My father hoped that perhaps, once we arrived at the station and showed our papers, they may let us return home and not be put on the train. My mother would hide in the attic of the apartment and the two of us would go as ordered.

I said goodbye to my mother, not realizing this would be the last time I would see her. I think often what I would have said to her had I known this. The pain still brings tears to my eyes when I think of that moment. It reinforces the wisdom of cherishing every moment with your loved ones. Everything was happening so quickly at this moment, that I can't remember my emotions or what I said to her.

My father and I left the apartment and headed toward the station. As we turned the corner onto one of the main streets, we saw hordes of people moving in the same direction. Soldiers and policemen shouted and pushed them forward at gunpoint. The situation was becoming chaotic. Old men and women who could barely walk, the sick and lame, young children and babies in their mother's arms were being shoved along mercilessly.

As we got nearer to the station, we could see the railcars and people being forced into them. There was no evidence that anyone was allowed to return to their homes in the ghetto. My father realized that the papers we carried would do us no good. At that point, he grabbed my arm and pulled me with him quickly and quietly into an alley way. Now out of sight, we ran and turned onto another street. Just down the street was a lumberyard. We darted inside and found a stack of lumber to crouch behind.

Outside, pandemonium was erupting. Shouts and screams and cries for mercy echoed across the city buildings. Then gunfire began to ricochet through the streets. The barking of trained dogs blended with the cries of children. My father told me to lie down and stay as still as possible. It was early, but already the day was getting warm. The smell of the lumber filled my nostrils and the pounding of my heart blocked out some of the awful noises outside. What was next for us?

AKTION! DEATH COMES TO CZESTOCHOWA
SEPTEMBER 1942

A stream of tacky, golden-brown resin hung bulbously from the stack of lumber just above my nose. I stared at it imagining that it was honey, but that would only intensify the pain of thirst and hunger in my throat and stomach. For hours it did not noticeably move although gravity was clearly pulling it downward. My nostrils were filled with the pungent and familiar smell of fresh-cut boards. I also knew the taste of resin and realized that it was not pleasant, even though it looked sweet. As I looked up at the resin, the memory of eating golden honey dripping from a slice of freshly baked bread filled my head and made me dizzy.

My father and I had been hiding in the lumberyard all day. We had scurried into it to escape the onslaught of the Nazi raid. Once inside, we crawled under a stack of lumber to get out of sight. While we lay motionless for hours, shots rang out from the nearby Jewish ghetto of Częstochowa, Poland. The Nazis had come to kill all its Jews in what was callously called a "liquidation." That frightful day in September 1942 would send me on a long and desperate journey and a fight for survival.

Częstochowa, my hometown, was bigger than a shtetl or even a town. In fact, it was a city and was quite well known as a holy city for Catholics. In the Jasna Góra Monastery in the city is the world-famous painting of the Black Madonna. According to tradition, it was brought to Częstochowa in 1384 by the Duke of Opole, a city in Southern Poland. Millions of Catholics make pilgrimages to see the painting every year. Pope John Paul II revealed that he had secretly visited the painting, at considerable risk, during World War II while the Nazis controlled the region.

Despite its place in the Catholic faith, there was quite a large Jewish community in Częstochowa before the war. That was about to change dramatically. Operation Reinhard had begun. It was the Nazi plan to eliminate all the Jews in Poland.

The smell of the lumber and the oozing resin was very familiar to me. My father had owned a lumberyard in Częstochowa. When the Germans invaded Poland in 1939, it did not take them long to seize his business and force him to house German soldiers and officials who came to rule the area. Now, ironically, he and I were hiding among the lumber to escape the murderers. This was not his lumberyard, but another one in a different part of town. It was familiar all the same.

Once the liquidation had ended, the vast majority of all those people had been sent to death camps, most of them to Treblinka. Here on this dark day, I waited under the stacks of wood wondering what my fate would be.

My father and I were fortunate not to be discovered. The chaos that ensued in the streets outside was loud and furious. With each shot, my body pulsed and twitched. The sound of them was frightening, and the screams and cries of our fellow Jews were horrifying. But there was a sound more petrifying to me at that moment. Nearby and in the distance, dozens of dogs barked frantically as they sniffed out people hiding and fleeing from the Nazis. What chance could we have if they came near us?

As the hours passed, the noise of terror rose and fell throughout like winds in a violent storm.

My father was a hard worker and had built his business from the ground up with much sacrifice. For my mother and me he had made a wonderful and comfortable life in a world which was still reeling from the Great Depression. We were not rich by any means, yet we had everything we needed and much more. While it wasn't large, our home was comfortable and big enough for the three of us. It was a modest but nice apartment in a residential building near the center of town. Every summer, we took a long holiday at various resorts in the Caucasus Mountains in Southeast Poland. Very often, only my mother and my aunts would go because my father had to stay and take care of the business.

Perhaps my father would be disappointed, but those summer vacation trips were the time of year I looked forward to most. Perhaps he would have preferred me to say the Jewish Holy Days were my favorite. While not Orthodox, he was a religious man and kept the traditions of our faith very carefully. His store was closed every Sabbath and during the holy days. Sabbath evenings were always a delightful time, with candles lit and a prayer offered up as it began. We had a kosher home.

He did not wear a beard or have unshaven locks. However, my grandfathers were both Hasidic and did maintain that tradition. The rules in their homes were much more traditional and we honored that when we visited. My father chose to be more modern in his lifestyle and to blend a bit more into Polish society.

As I lay under the lumber, I tried to think of the happy times we spent with our grandparents to keep me from going into a complete panic. I tried hard to keep my breathing normal and to be as still as possible. It was becoming more and more difficult as the commotion in the streets continued.

Eventually, the late afternoon sun gave way to dusk and gradually the pandemonium died down. The shooting stopped, except for an occasional burst from far away. The dogs had been taken away and silenced and that gave me a great sense of relief.

We waited patiently until nightfall finally came. Underneath the boards, I could see almost nothing. A nearby streetlight shone just brightly enough to reveal the way out of the lumberyard. My father beckoned me to follow him, and the two of us quietly and cautiously emerged from our hiding place. We moved slowly to the entrance and then into the darkened street.

My father said we would try to get back to our house and hopefully find my mother there to be reunited. It wasn't far, but it was now past curfew and if a Jew was caught out after that they would be shot on sight. Even though it was quiet, and the killing had stopped, policemen and soldiers were still patrolling the area. This section of the city was now deserted, perhaps because it had just been made *Judenrein* or "rid of Jews."

My father knew the streets very well and he took a route that weaved in and out of the buildings and along the sides of them rather than directly down the street. We moved carefully from building to building until we came very close to our house. Just a couple of yards to cross and we would be home.

As we moved through one of those lots, my father spotted a water faucet protruding from the back of a house. We were both so thirsty and extremely dehydrated. He had brought a bottle filled with tea when we left home that morning. Now it was empty. He went over to the faucet and began to fill the bottle.

Suddenly, a Polish policeman was staring my father in the face. Where had he come from so quickly? It may have been the sound of the water beginning to flow that tipped him off. I jumped in terror and my whole body tensed up. I was beginning to panic, but I managed to calm myself for the moment. The policeman demanded to know what we were doing there and why we were out after curfew. His gun was pointed directly at my father as he questioned him.

That morning, when we left our house, my father had taken out some money from his pocket, had given it to me, and had told me to hide it in my shoe. Now he begged the policeman not to take us away, and said he would give him our money. He then turned to me and told me to get it and give it to the man. I began to reach for my shoe as my father began to take off his watch from his wrist. "Here, take my watch too," he told the officer.

The officer was not to be bribed, at least not so easily. "Just wait here," he commanded, turned and went back out to the street. Why he left was unclear to me. Was he going to get help or was he just checking to make sure no other policemen would see him take the bribe?

Either way, with him now out of sight, I felt an overwhelming urge to run. I turned and darted across the yard and did not stop until I reached the yard of our apartment building just a short distance away. I did not dare go into the house, since I did not know who might be waiting for me there. So, I hid under some bushes at the edge of the lot and waited.

In my panic to get away, I had not said a word to my father. I did not ask him if I should run. Even now, remembering the incident, I cannot understand why I took flight. What was I thinking, as a 12-year-old girl, abandoning my father in such a dangerous situation? It was just an instinct, perhaps out of desperation, panic, and fear. I know I was feeling all of those and looking back now, I realize running would be a natural response to them. I began to fear for my father's safety and waited in the dark hoping he would soon join me.

As the long, nervous moments crept by and the noise of more policemen coming to join the search for us increased, I began to realize I would not see him very soon. I did everything I could to hold back my sobs and tears as I lay motionless in the cool fall air of the September night.

RANSACKED!
SEPTEMBER 1942

I lay motionless under the bush and tried to look through the branches and the darkness to see any signs of life in my house. It was only a few feet away, but after what we witnessed in the town that day, I was afraid to go inside without investigating more fully. I wondered if my father had been able to get away from the policeman. I began to feel guilty for having abandoned him.

The night was cooling fast, and I was shivering. Perhaps it was more from fear than from cold because the weather was still relatively warm for late September. The sounds of the policemen searching finally died down and stopped. Just to be sure I still waited.

My mind wandered back to my early childhood. I remembered the joy of going to school and the excitement of learning new things. I loved to read about history. I attended a traditional Jewish school and naturally we learned about our faith's forefathers. The stories were so dramatic and powerful and had survived the test of time. We read about how Abraham had been willing to offer his son Isaac in sacrifice and was spared at the last moment by God from this test of obedience. How Moses had given up his powerful place in the mighty Egyptian kingdom to defend one of his Jewish brothers from being beaten to death. He was forced to flee Egypt and live in the wilderness eventually returning to lead his people out of slavery and into the promised land. How the Babylonians had captured Jerusalem and taken the Jews back to their capital city and made them slaves once again. And all about the miracle of the oil lamp when the Seleucid king, Antiochus Epiphanes, tried to eradicate the Jewish faith in the 2nd century, B.C.E.

Why had Jews been so hated and targeted throughout history? How could it be happening again?

We also studied Western history in school. I knew there had been many attempts over the past 2,000 years by despots who wanted to conquer and rule all of Europe. From the Roman Caesars to Charlemagne and from Napoleon to Kaiser Wilhelm, war descended on the continent as these dictators tried to erase national and tribal borders and create a single European culture. What was happening now was monumentally different. This new tyrant, Adolph Hitler, was truly an insane madman. How the German people could acquiesce and allow him to come to power puzzled us all. Once again, the Jews were squarely in the sights of an evil man's wrath.

My mind drifted away from my school lessons and onto the good times I had with my neighbor friends. We did not have TV or video games. Our times were spent outside in the streets, the parks, and the fields. We played tag, hopscotch, and jumped rope. In the fields we played soccer and chased each other in games of keep away. All that was gone now. To be outside at all in the last year was to risk being captured or killed. And now, thinking about me being outside, after curfew, and in an area that had just been cleared of Jews, my heart began to race again in fear.

How long had I been lying under the bush? It had been quiet for a long time, or so it seemed. I knew I could not stay there all night and certainly not once the sun began to come up. I had lost track of time. Perhaps the sun would be rising soon? I suddenly felt the urgency to move on.

The house had been completely silent and dark the entire time I hid in the yard. I decided to move carefully and slowly toward it. Out from under bush, I approached the house and around to the front door, all the while listening and looking for any movement. The wind suddenly stirred the trees. It did so gently, but it was enough to jolt me and cause me to stop. I looked around and saw no one nearby. The street was empty. I hurried up to the open door and stepped inside out of sight. As I moved into the main room, my eyes adjusted to the blackness of the night.

There, to my horror, I saw the house had been ransacked. Furniture was overturned, lamps and other household items were strewn across the floor. In the kitchen, pots and pans were scattered, dishes lay smashed and broken, and the cupboard doors stood open. I moved a little further toward the bedroom. Suddenly I stopped, frozen in my tracks, paralyzed. A horrible thought had gripped me and prevented me from moving a muscle. I could only imagine that the next thing I would see would be my mother lying dead on the floor.

I straightened up in panic, and stepped backward. Then I turned and ran out into the street, determined to get as far away from the house as I could.

ON THE EDGE OF THE GHETTO
SEPTEMBER 1942

As I left the ransacked house and made my way back out into the dark and now silent streets, I had no idea what to do next. It was a long time past the curfew, and I knew there would be no mercy for me if I was seen.

I did my best to stay in the shadows and away from any lights. I once again strengthened my resolve to remain calm and think clearly. Where did this determination spring from? I had been a pampered only child. A little girl raised protected in every way from the harshness that life could bring. Surely what I had witnessed and experienced during the past two years since the Nazis had brought their terror, had contributed to my toughening. I still ponder how such a young 12-year-old could muster up the will to continue.

My mind raced with fear but also with urgency to find safety. Where could I go to hide and wait for the daylight to end the curfew and allow me to find my father. Was the terror over that the previous day had brought? I was not optimistic. I decided it would be best to return to the bushes in the garden and wait for morning.

I crawled back under the prickly branches of the shrubs and lay down. My heart pounded so loudly that it was difficult to think. I searched my memory deeply to remember the layout of the town. Our house was on the very edge of the Jewish ghetto. On one side was a railroad track that separated the ghetto from the Polish neighborhood. A fence enclosed our property from the tracks. On one side, there was a gate that opened to the railway line. Maybe if I could get into the Polish side of town, I could blend in or hide there until I could find my father.

Suddenly, I remembered that not too far from our house, on the Polish side, was a grocery store owned by a very nice Polish lady. My mother used to buy food from her and she always friendly and treated us kindly. Now I had a plan. But it would have to wait for the morning since any attempt during the curfew could be the end of me. I relaxed a bit and took a deep breath. I lay under the leaves of the bush and prayed. I tried to sleep. Even though I was feeling calmer and was exhausted, sleep would not come.

The hours slowly passed and eventually the light of dawn was filling the sky. I waited patiently until I could hear the town come alive and the movement of the people began to increase. Now it was fully light, and I carefully emerged from the bushes and started to make my way to the gate.

As I took the first few steps, my right leg almost collapsed under me. I looked down and saw that I only had one shoe. Incredibly, I had gone through the night forgetting that I had taken off my right shoe to get the money for my father to give the policeman. It was precisely at that moment that I darted away from them both and fled to my house, leaving my shoe with my father. It was too hard to walk with just one shoe, so I took off the left one and continued barefooted toward the fence.

At the gate, I carefully looked through to see what was on the other side. Just beyond the train tracks was an embankment that rose into the Polish neighborhood. Because it was the boundary to the ghetto, policemen were deployed along the top of the embankment to keep a watch for Jews trying to leave the ghetto. I waited and watched carefully to see if any were nearby. In a few moments, one appeared and slowly walked along the edge glancing toward the ghetto and down the railway. He stopped and turned toward the gate where I was crouched. Had he seen me? I ducked down lower and away from the opening from which I peered. I waited for a few minutes and tried not to make a sound.

When I finally got the nerve to look again, he was gone. Relieved, I slowly stood back up and checked the gate. It was locked and I couldn't force it open. I would have to climb over it to get to the other side. Would I have enough time before the policeman returned? I didn't know, but I could not continue to stay in the garden. Without a further thought I scrambled up and over the gate and down the other side. How had I done it? I was a tiny little girl and the gate seemed so high. Yet somehow, I was over and on the other side. No time to waste, I scrambled up and over the embankment and started on my way to the store of our Polish friend.

Would she be there? Could I make it there without being caught? Would she help me, or would she be too frightened? So many questions and only one way to answer them—to continue and try my best not to be seen or noticed.

The streets were coming alive and there were a few people moving about. I was very close to the store now. Once again, I mustered up all the resolve I could to try and remain calm. My heart pounded so hard that I thought it was going to explode out of my chest. I wanted to run as fast as I could, but I kept my head enough to maintain a normal pace. I did not want to draw attention to myself if anyone should see me. I turned the corner down the street that led to the store. Just a few more steps to determine if my hope for help from this woman who had been so friendly and helpful to us was justified.

Memories of going to the store with my mother raced through my mind as I tried to build my courage for approaching her. During the difficult times in the ghetto, this woman had helped us many times. When we could not pay for food, she had given some to us anyway. My mother did her best to pay what she could, but sometimes she had nothing. Even when she did pay for the food, Ms. Sporna would often give her extra sugar or bread or potatoes. We were so grateful for her kindness especially since she put herself at risk to do so.

After the Germans began to confiscate valuables from the Jews, it became even more difficult to find ways to pay for the things we needed. They demanded jewelry, gold, and silver be given over to help their war effort. When the order came down for all Jews to turn in their fur coats, my mother determined that she would give her coat directly to this friend. She would rather her have it than for the Germans to get it. My father also had a fur-lined coat, and she gave her that also. They were both very valuable coats.

As I thought about the coats, I wondered if she still had them. After spending a whole night out in the cold air, I imagined the feeling of having one to keep me warm. I wondered if she might pity me enough to give one of them back to me. Right now, I just needed to be hidden and maybe a little bite to eat. I didn't anticipate any more than that from her. At the very least, I hoped that she would not turn me in to the police. As nice as she had been to us, I was not sure. Instead of getting the help I needed, this might be the end for me.

MS. SPORNA
SEPTEMBER 1942

I knew the way to the Polish grocery store very well. It was still early and not many people were out in the streets yet. I began to become very frightened that I would be noticed. I had no shoes. My clothing was tattered. Someone would surely know I did not belong on the Polish side. And, of course, I had a very Jewish look. My hair was dark. My eyes were dark. My features were obviously Semitic. We had lived alongside the Poles for a long time, and they could tell if a person was Jewish by all these things.

I knew I must do something to deflect any suspicion and hide my growing nervousness. Almost without thinking, I began to skip, as if I was on my way to the park to play with my friends. I tried to whistle, thinking this would also give the appearance that I was a happy and normal little Polish girl enjoying the new day. But I could not get a sound out of my lips. My mouth was dry, and my lips chapped from being out all night. My heart pounded as I thought about what a sight I must be. I was sure I was failing at this attempted ruse.

All of sudden, my fears were confirmed; I heard footsteps behind me. I was being followed by a Polish man. I turned my head to one side, trying to catch a view of him with my peripheral vision, careful not to turn fully around. I was filled with panic, yet somehow, I managed to hide it. I dared not look back too long and quickly fixed my gaze in front of me continuing my skipping pace toward the Polish woman's house.

It was of no use. The man had recognized me. Softly he called out to me, "Żydóweczko!" This was Polish for, "Little Jewish girl!" When I heard that word, it was like an electric shock pulsed through my whole body. I expected any second to be grabbed by my hair and dragged to the police. I had seen them do this to other Jewish women and girls. Now it was my turn.

He said it again, "Little Jewish girl!" This time much more quietly. In almost a whisper he continued, "You better run, because they are going to catch you!" I looked back at him again but this time directly at his face. He raised his hand and motioned me forward as if shooing me away.

He knew exactly who I was or, more correctly perhaps, what I was. A great feeling of relief came over me. This man was not going to report me or turn me over to the authorities. He was sincerely warning me and urged me to find a place to hide quickly. I stopped my skipping and broke into a full run. I was now only a few yards away from the store. I rushed up to the door and knocked several times. If the knocking matched the pounding of my heart, it could have knocked the door down.

In a few minutes, our family friend stood in the open doorway. Her face went pale, and she slapped her hand to her chest. Her mouth dropped open. She could not believe that I was there. She quickly recovered, grabbed me by the arm, and pulled me inside. Just as quickly, she slammed the door shut and locked it securely.

"My dear Halina! Where have you come from?" she gasped. "Where are your shoes? You are so dirty, and you look exhausted!"

"Ms. Sporna. I am so tired. And so thirsty. Can you give me some water?" I pleaded.

She took me into the kitchen, sat me in a chair and poured the water. After I gulped it down, she put a kettle of water on the stove to make me a hot drink. I told her the story and asked if she could please help me. She began to prepare some food.

I could see the fear in her eyes as she realized what this act of kindness could mean for her. But she said nothing. She put the food in front of me and I almost inhaled it. After a few minutes, she said to me. "Let's clean you up and then you can get some rest. I will think about what we should do after that."

I thanked her profusely and went to the bathroom to clean up.

"YOU CANNOT STAY"
SEPTEMBER 1942

Someone is calling my name. Is this still the dream? My eyes slowly opened, and I saw I on was on a bed in Ms. Sporna's house. I tried to clear the sleepiness from my head and remember why I was here. The fear and terror of the past few days rushed back in my mind. I prayed that perhaps it was all just a dream and that I would soon be back to a normal life with my mother and father at my home.

"Halina," Ms. Sporna whispered. "Wake up dear. I need to talk to you."

I could see that the sunlight had diminished, and the room was growing dark. The last few rays of light blinked through the curtains on the window. Now I was fully awake, and my heart sank as I realized it had not been a dream. I had been running for my life and found my way to our dear friend's house. She had been so kind to take me in and give me something to eat, clean up and rest. I had slept for some time, but it was not a fulfilling sleep. I knew I had tossed and turned and perhaps had been only dozing. I could remember sounds from the street and the store in the next room as her customers had come and gone.

"Halina," she continued, "I am afraid to keep you here. I am not just afraid for myself. I am afraid for you too. I am quite certain they will eventually find you and that will be death for both of us."

I listened quietly. Her words were painfully logical, and I knew she was right. Fear began to well up inside me. I sat up and looked at her. "I know you are right," I acknowledged. "But where can I go? I will have to hide. They are probably searching for me already since I ran away from the policeman and my father."

"Maybe you can find your father?" she questioned. "Perhaps he has returned to your house."

"Perhaps," I said, "but I do not think so. I was outside our apartment all night, and no one came back. Not my father and not my mother. I am so afraid they have been taken away, or worse they are... And I am too afraid to go back to the apartment for fear that the police will be waiting for me. And if not, they will surely come again to look."

"I understand," Ms. Sporna said, "but you must go, they will certainly find you here eventually."

She turned and went into the store where she gathered some food and other things for me to take with me. She put them in a bag and handed them to me. In the bag was a loaf of bread and some hard-boiled eggs. She found a bottle and filled it with tea and closed its cap. Then she went back into the store for a few minutes and returned with some wooden shoes that were close to my size. She beckoned me to try them on. They were not an exact fit, but I could walk in them without too much trouble. This would be better than going barefoot.

I picked up the bag of food and thanked her again for her help and all she had done for me. We talked some more while we waited for it to get completely dark. Then I stepped out into the night. The darkness engulfed me and temporary blindness it brought I found strangely comforting. I knew it would also keep me from being seen. And what was the point of seeing when one does not know which way to turn anyway? Why see the way forward when you don't know which way is forward?

In my uncertainty I kept moving in the random direction I had chosen. Now a sense of panic started to return. Should I run? Should I crouch in the bushes again and wait? Why had I run away from my father that evening? It would have been better for me to have been caught with him and to be with him now, no matter where he had been taken or what had been his fate. At least I would not be alone. I imagined several other terrible scenarios that could be my fate. The panic was growing.

With that I stopped suddenly. I gathered my thoughts and told myself to put the fear out of my mind. I must think clearly. I had not walked very far from the store. With a renewed focus, I listened carefully to hear if there was anyone around. Then I began to move forward again, more slowly this time, not wanting the wooden clogs to make too much noise.

Suddenly, I remembered the most famous place in Częstochowa— the Jasna Góra monastery. This is where the famous painting of the Black Madonna was kept. At the monastery was a cloister and I thought that might be a good place to hide, especially at night. It was not too far from here. I started toward it and tried hard not to run because of the noisy clogs. I am certain I walked too fast since I was so anxious to get there before I encountered anyone else in the street.

It took only a few minutes to arrive at the church. It seemed much longer as I expected to be seen and captured with every corner turned. Now in front of the church, I stopped and looked carefully all around. It was all quiet and nothing moved. I went inside and found a place to hide.

I started to relax knowing I was alone here. I found a place to lie down and try to sleep. Then I remembered something that began to make me nervous once again. Today was Saturday. In the morning there would be people coming to Mass. I tried to calm myself and sleep, but the uncertainty of where I would go next had me wide awake. Where would I go? I had no plan. There was no way to make a plan. The only thing for certain was that I would have to get away before the church services started. I may have dozed off a few times that evening, but I did not sleep.

ALONE ON THE RUN
SEPTEMBER 1942

The church had been empty and silent all night except for the usual creaks of such an old building. Every little sound jolted me and put me on edge. It was still dark when I emerged from the last bit of dozing. What time was it? I did not know, but I knew I had been there many hours already and it must be close to dawn. I decided it was time to get away before anyone came to the church on this Sunday morning.

I eased my way outside the churchyard and into the street. I started walking down the road away from the town. I had decided it was best to get away from Częstochowa because there was more of a chance to be caught there. Perhaps I could find a small village nearby where I could hide. That was the extent of my plan. Just keep walking and looking for places to hide. I was at the mercy now of fate and luck. I tried then to stop thinking and just move forward.

I walked for a few kilometers and came upon a village. Daylight was beginning to fill the sky. It was Sunday morning, and the village was still quiet as the residents took advantage of their day of rest. I approached it very cautiously and kept my eyes and ears wide open for any signs of life. As I got to the edge of the town, I was relieved to see that not a soul was outside. Encouraged, I entered the village and looked around.

During these times, Polish villages looked very much like what you would see in story books with tales from days of old. Not much changed in them for hundreds of years and so far the technological advancements of the 20th century had not changed this one. Down this little road were maybe 15 to 20 little houses, all with thatched roofs and tiny gardens. Suddenly, one of the houses caught my eye. It was burned out and clearly abandoned. Maybe this could be a good hiding place. I ran to it and looked inside.

The walls of the house were gone from the fire, but its frame still held the roof in place. The ceiling was also still intact and on one end a brick chimney stood as solidly as when it was first constructed. I could see there was an attic above the ceiling, a perfect place to hide. No one could see from outside and hopefully no one would be coming to the house since it had been deserted. But how could I get up there without stairs or ladder. The only way to reach the attic would be to climb the chimney. I was a tiny girl and not very good at climbing. And to climb while holding the bag of food that I most desperately needed made the task impossible?

Not deterred, I went over the to the chimney to see if I could climb it. About halfway up the chimney I saw a horseshoe embedded in the brick. I noticed that the curve of the horseshoe stuck out just enough that something could be tied to it. Suddenly, an idea popped into my head. I had a belt on my dress. I hurriedly took it off and tied the bag of food to it. Then I took the other end of the belt and tied it to the horseshoe. Then somehow with strength and agility that I did not know I had, I scurried up the side of the chimney and into the attic. Once there, I reached down and grabbed the belt and pulled the bag of food into the attic. This good fortune and my ability to take advantage of it surprised me. I was so happy to be here, out of sight.

I looked around the attic and saw there was nothing except some straw. Another bit of good fortune because I could use the straw to make a comfortable place to sleep. It would also provide some warmth during the night. I breathed a huge sigh of relief and began to relax. I had not eaten for a long time because of the fear and anxiety. I did not even think about eating and had not felt my hunger pains. Now, with a feeling of safety, I was dizzy from the lack of food. I opened the bag and took out the bread and a boiled egg. I wanted to eat it all right then, but I knew I had to be disciplined and make it last as long as I could. I tore off a small piece of the bread and took a tiny bite. I peeled the egg and ate it all. Then I drank just a few sips of the tea. My thirst too was very strong, but I resisted the temptation to drink more. I put the cap back on the bottle and closed the bag. I lay down and closed my eyes. Maybe the sleep will help me forget my hunger. Before long I was in slumber. This was the safest I had felt since leaving my father. The sleep was deep and dreamless.

HIDING IN THE ATTIC
SEPTEMBER 1942

I awoke to a rooster crowing from across the street. At first, it jolted me and sent fear shooting through my body. Where was I? Was I safe? Had I fallen asleep from exhaustion somewhere out in the open? The fog of slumber quickly cleared, and I remembered my good fortune earlier that morning at finding this burned-out house and its attic still intact. With a sigh of relief, my thoughts turned to my intense hunger. My stomach growled and churned. My lips and tongue were sticky with dryness. I looked for the bottle of tea Ms. Sporza had given me. When I put it to my lips, I almost turned it upside down to empty it, but I found the willpower to resist and raised it just enough to let the tea touch my lips to moisten them. I stuck my tongue into the mouth of the bottle and then licked my lips. I did not know how long I could stay here, and I needed to preserve my food and the tea. I raised the bottle again and took a tiny sip. I did not swallow it immediately. Instead, I swirled it around in my mouth to wet my gums and the back of my throat. Then I let it trickle down my throat.

Reaching for my food, I noticed the boards of the walls in the attic were not tightly constructed. The morning light penetrated the narrow slits and painted a geometric pattern on the floor. Dust particles danced in the rays of sun. I wanted to eat a few more bites, but I could hear sounds coming from the house across the street. My curiosity could not wait, and I scooted over to the wall to peer through the cracks and down into the yard where the noises were coming from. I could see a family beginning their work in the garden and around the house. Several children dutifully carried out their chores in methodical and efficient silence. The children fed their chickens and gave water to the cow and goats. I watched with great interest as they busily went about the house.

There was something satisfying about seeing people living a normal life without fear for their lives. The scene entertained me and gave me a bit of relief from the terror I had been through over the past couple of days. Soon, their mother came out from the house and called them inside. I turned my gaze to the village further down the street. I could see people moving about but I could not see enough from this angle to determine what they did. It was Sunday, so the pace was casual and peaceful.

I returned to the bag of food and took out some bread and ate a small piece of it. Then I felt a great sense of relaxation and settled into a comfortable position to wait out the day. I tried my best to be still and silent so not to arouse any suspicion from passersby. My curiosity kept me watching the people in the village through the boards. I thought about a lot of things for the rest of the day—my home back in Częstochowa, my school friends, the wonderful vacations with my mother.

Remembering my mother caused sorrow and fear to well up inside me. What had happened to her? Had she gotten out of the house before it was ransacked? I prayed that she was still alive and OK. What had happened to my father? Had the policeman been merciful to him and spared his life? So many questions filled my head with doubt and uncertainty. I told myself to imagine the positive and not believe the negative. They may both still be alive, and we may be back together again soon. It was possible, so for now that is what I would believe. The day moved very slowly, but my meandering thoughts helped to speed up time. Once sunset had come, the night came quickly. I rearranged the straw in many different ways trying to make the most comfortable bed possible. Once I was satisfied, I lay down and before long I was fast asleep.

The next morning, I was jolted again by noises from across the street. This time however, it was much more frightening. There were a lot of people talking and I could hear metal clanking against metal. What was this commotion? Were the Germans here looking for Jews? I pulled myself as quietly as I could to the wall and looked through the crack. I was relieved to see that it was only Polish peasants from the town. They had come to dig potatoes in the field next to the house. Their shovels, rakes and hoes banged together as they carried them to begin their work.

I had slept surprisingly well all night long. I didn't remember waking at all. Was it because of the comfort of the straw or just complete exhaustion from the past days' events? A little of both, I suppose. I felt more rested than I had in many days. I watched for a few hours as the workers dug their potatoes and piled them into baskets. The children worked alongside the adults and seemed to be just as efficient.

As the sun crested in the noon-day sky, the laborers stopped for rest and a bit of food. A couple of the men walked toward the house in which I hid. They were seeking some shade from the bright warm sun. They stopped when they got under the attic and talked in tones too soft for me to understand. Suddenly, I heard one of them say. "I wonder if there is anything in the attic above." The other one seemed just as curious and replied, "Let's go up and see."

My heart skipped a beat. Quickly, I scooted away from the opening near the chimney and into a dark corner. I curled up to make myself as small as possible and hoped that the dim light would prevent them from seeing me. They were much better at climbing the chimney than I had been and in a split second they were both standing at the other side of the attic. At first, they stood still and silent and made no attempt to approach me. I prayed that they would realize there was nothing here of value and go back down. They were only waiting for their eyes to adjust to the darkness. It only took a moment before they spotted me.

"Who are you?" one of them demanded. "What are you doing here?" he continued.

I began to shiver with fear and thought quickly about what to answer. I had not spoken out loud for a long time and with my parched throat, I struggled to get any words out. Somehow my voice began to work. I decided that I would try my best to convince them that I was Polish. "I am a Polish girl from Częstochowa. Something happened to my parents. I don't know where they are. I have been looking for them all over, but when it got dark last night, I decided to sleep here." I do not remember what I babbled next, a few other poorly made-up details that did not add up.

They looked at me with incredulity. Clearly, they did not believe me. "You are lying!" one of them shouted. "You are a Jewish girl and you have run away to hide."

His words sent shockwaves of fear through my body, but the tone of his voice was more frightening. It was not friendly. He looked at me for a few seconds.

I stayed silent and did not answer. I knew it was futile to protest. I began to shake as I realized my alibi had been so weak.

Then something unexpected happened. The second man stepped forward and bent down toward me. "Don't worry dear girl. It's alright. We are not going to harm you," he said in soothing tones. "I suppose you are fleeing the aktion in Częstochowa?"

I nodded my head sheepishly.

"We were there when it was taking place," he continued. "It was terrible. Many people were killed and many more were rounded up and sent away by train. But some others were captured and are being held in the movie theater. There are a few hundred we have been told. They are keeping them to use them as forced laborers." He told me the location and I remembered where it was. As I think back on that exchange, it was not necessary for him to tell me this, but it would come in handy for me in a few days.

"Anyway, you can stay here and hide for a while. We will not tell anyone you are here," the man finished.

Then the other one said, "We will bring you some food too. We will do what we can to help you."

Was I still dreaming? Could this good fortune be true? I thought about pinching myself to see if I would wake. But I knew I was not asleep. The rollercoaster of emotions that I had just ridden through in these few minutes was overtaking me. I could not answer because the feeling of relief had paralyzed my mouth and tongue. Finally, I somehow managed to utter a weak thankyou. My whole body suddenly relaxed as the fear and anxiety fled my mind. I took in a deep breath and let it out quickly. Then my body began to tremble with relief. Such a wave of conflicting emotions in just a few short minutes had exhausted me. I felt dizzy and I leaned back against the wall to steady myself.

The men descended back down the chimney and I watched them through the boards as they made their way back to the house. I was still in disbelief. And suddenly the doubts and fears returned. Were they being honest with me? Perhaps they only said this to keep me here while they alert the authorities to come and take me away. This scenario was not uncommon. Many times, the local Poles had promised to help Jews, only to turn them over for a reward or after their fear of being caught became too great. I was not ready to accept my good fortune so quickly. This awful fight for my life against these evil murderers was teaching me to be very untrusting. Should I run away while they are gone? I knew this was futile too so for now, I waited to see what manner of men these were.

It did not take long for me to find out. In just a short while, one of the men returned and brought me some boiled potatoes. I thanked him profusely. He nodded graciously and said that he would be back later at the end of the day to check on me. The potatoes were still steaming from the boiling water. I ate them so fast that I scorched my tongue and the roof of my mouth. My throat ached as the partially chewed bits passed through too quickly. Yet, I don't remember a more delicious meal.

The men were good to their word and more so. That evening, after the children had been put to bed and were asleep, the man from the house across the street came back. He brought a ladder and put it in place and climbed up. He told me to come down with him. He took me to the house and introduced me to his wife. My tattered and filthy clothes must have stirred her. She looked at me with great pity, then took my hand and led me to the bathroom. "Wash up as best you can my dear. Take your time, but try to be quiet so you don't wake the children. We do not want them to know you are here because they may say something to someone who is not happy for you to be here." She closed the door and I cleaned up.

After I was cleaned, they gave me a bit more food and something warm to drink. It was so refreshing to be clean again and not so hungry. After I ate, they hurried me out, concerned that too much time there increased the chance of being seen. The man came with me bringing the ladder so I could get into the attic for the night. We carefully and quietly crossed the road. I ascended the ladder and thanked him silently. That night's sleep was even more peaceful and fulfilling than the night before.

DIE ALONE OR DIE WITH MY PEOPLE?

SEPTEMBER 1942

I went in and out of sleep through the night and my mind found it difficult to distinguish my dreams from reality. I could now see the first signs of light and I remembered where I was again. The attic of this burned-out house was primitive, but it had provided me some respite of safety from the fear I had faced over the past week. This morning marked one week of living here. These peasants had been so kind to me and brought me three meals every day. They were meager, but it was better than I had eaten in a long time.

Now I heard them coming again but this time the sound was different. There was urgency in their voices and there seemed to be an unusual commotion brewing. My protector's face appeared at the opening of the attic, and it was filled with dread.

"The Germans are coming, and they are looking everywhere for Jews who have run away," he said in a shaky voice. "I am so afraid that they will find you here. And, if they do, they will kill you I am certain. I am also afraid for my family. I hate to tell you this, but you must leave."

I did not know what to answer, but I knew he was right. These people had been so kind to me, I could not ask them to risk their lives for me now. Where would I go now? All my options were disappearing. I did not have the energy or courage to continue fleeing.

I remembered what he had told me about some of the Jews in Częstochowa being kept there for labor and not sent away to the death camps. Perhaps I could go and join them. Once again, I had come to the point of preferring to die with my people than to endure the trauma of constantly being on the run. This is what I would do. But could I get back to the city without being caught? They were already looking for me I thought. If I am seen that will be the end of me. On the other hand, if I could get back undetected, perhaps I could slip into the movie theater where the Jews were being kept and blend in as if I had been there all the time.

In my mind, it was not a hard decision. I could no longer take the unbearable stress of trying to hide. If they caught me, so be it. Better a quick death than waiting for it to come in such uncertainty. I grabbed my few belongings and thanked the man for his kindness. I could see the relief in his eyes at my decision to go. He said something about not wanting to see me get killed. His words indicated concern for me, but his inflection made me realize his concern was mostly for his family and himself. He was terribly afraid that he would be killed for helping me and I understood.

The morning sun was growing brighter now as I moved down the road toward the city. More people were starting their day and with every person I saw my fear grew. But so far, I did not see any German soldiers. I moved as fast as I could without drawing too much attention to myself. I knew the way to this theater very well. I chose a route that I thought would be the least busy.

Eventually, I came to the place. Outside was a water wagon and the Jews were coming out to drink from it. I slipped into the flow of pedestrians on the street and moved toward the theater. As we moved past the water wagon, I ducked down and took a place amidst the workers.

I had made it completely unnoticed and now stood with my fellow Jews. I looked around. I recognized a few faces, but so far, no one had recognized me. A great relief overcame me to once again be a Jew among everyone else. In a moment, some of the Jews saw that I did not have the yellow armband required for Jews. Somehow, very quickly, one of them produced one for me and quickly wrapped it around my arm. Now I was fully integrated without suspicion.

By now, many of them had recognized me and were very glad to see that I was still alive. One of them pulled me into their work group. In a few minutes, they brought us a small piece of bread and then we were marched toward the center of town. Eventually, we arrived at a park and were instructed clean it. Some raked leaves, others picked up trash, while others dug trenches in the ground.

I was so happy to be "safe" with my people that my energy level soared. I was given a rake and I worked like I had never worked before. Where that energy came from, I cannot explain. It felt like I was on drugs. I worked so fast and furious that some of the other workers came to me to calm me down. They told me to take it easy and not exhaust myself. All I could think of was the emotional release of not having to flee and hide anymore. I could not slow myself and continued to work quickly.

No longer would I have to think about where to go next or what lay ahead in the road. No more worrying if anyone would help me and, if they did, would they eventually be found out or perhaps turn me in. No thoughts about where the next bit of food would come from. No more sleeping outside. And now I was once again with people. Not that being alone was the worst of it. I could have taken the solitude if I had known I could survive. But the odds had dwindled trying to do that on my own. Now I thought, it would be better to go with them on the trains to the gas chambers than to wait slowly for death in some uncertain and equally painful fashion.

The day of work finally ended, and we returned to the movie theater. I walked and saw scores of people lying down in rows preparing for sleep. The floor was mostly bare. In some places, there was straw. I could only find an empty spot with no straw. A few minutes later, a man came over to me and said, "You just came here today, didn't you?" I told him that was true. "Where are you from?" he continued. I told him and then he asked my name. My answer startled him. He excitedly said, "Wait here," and then left to go to the other side of the theater.

I was puzzled but waited in anticipation for his return. In a few minutes he came back. He crouched down next to me and, with a broad smile on his face, he whispered, "Your father is here!"

SEEING FATHER ONE LAST TIME
OCTOBER 1942

"My father! He is here!"

"Shhhh," the man said, pressing his finger to his lips.

"Where is he? Please, take me to him," I said, managing to suppress my excitement into softer tones.

"No, you must not go to him just yet," he warned. "He was also so happy to hear that you are here and OK, but he is afraid that it will create a commotion if you are seen with him. He is afraid that someone may denounce you to the guards if they see this."

I was crushed because I so wanted to see him immediately. My father's courage had been wrecked by the events of the past two years. At the same time, his paranoia intensified. Everything had been taken from him. All the hard work building up a successful business from nothing. I remembered back in the ghetto how he could hardly bring himself to leave the house out of fear. And the few times that he did, he always returned shaking and worrying that he was being followed and that someone was just ready to capture him and take him away. After the war started, my mother became the strength of the family. She found ways to get us food, clothing, and the other things we needed. My father could not find the resolve to overcome his fears. Now that fear prevented us from seeing one another.

The man saw the disappointment in my face as I realized I could not go to my father. "If you go now, everyone will see and notice. He is right. It is best to wait for the morning, after we go out to the work detail. You will be outside, and people will be going off to their jobs. Then you can go to him more in secret and fewer people will notice," he said, trying to comfort me.

His words were not that comforting, but I understood. The rest of the night was filled with anxiety. The joy of knowing he was alive, and that I would see him again welled up in my chest and gladdened me. At the same time, the pain of waiting through the night was tearing at my heart. I did not sleep much, tossing and turning on the cold hard floor. I imagined what I would say to him when we finally met, and I imagined what he would say to me. I hoped that he would say that my mother was also there, or at least somewhere safe. So many things to tell him and so many things to hear from him.

In the past year, I had experienced many nights that moved all too slowly. This one was one of the slowest. Finally, morning came. I was wide awake before the first rays of light entered the theater. A few people were beginning to mill about and prepare to go out for work. The sun broke over the horizon and, at last, it was time to go outside to be assigned our work. Once in the streets, I looked desperately for him. I spotted a man across the way who also seemed to be searching the crowd. Our eyes met and I tried my best not to run to him. He stood and waited for me as my legs staggered in their attempt to slow my gate. Now I was in front of him, and I tried hard to hold back my tears. We gave each other a quick hug but ended it almost immediately so as not to draw too much attention.

We spoke in hushed tones as we told each other what had happened over the past few days since we were parted. The words I imagined he would tell me about my mother did not come. Instead, he told me that she had been captured the night I ran away. Had I continued through our ransacked house that evening, I would not have found my mother lying dead. She had already been taken earlier in the day to train station and put on a train bound for a camp. We did not know which one she had been sent to. Most of those sent to death camps from Częstochowa were sent to Treblinka, not as well-known as Auschwitz, but just as deadly and evil. Now it did not matter. We would never see her again.

We waited anxiously for our daily work assignments. For some reason, today it was taking much longer to get them. What was happening? Soon, we learned that the Germans were going to take more of us away to the death camps and they would be coming any minute to make the selection. My father gasped in fear when he heard the news. His fear was not for himself but for me; I was so young and small. The young were considered too weak to do adequate work and were often the first to be sent to the death camps.

Quickly, my father looked around to find a woman who might have some makeup. If I put on some rouge and eyeliner he thought that would make me look older. Amazingly, he did find someone to help, and I quickly painted my face. He told me to stand as tall as I could to look older and healthier. I stretched myself up onto my tiptoes.

Soon, German soldiers arrived and began to separate the men from the women. My father and I were forced apart. I moved into the middle of the women and tried to hide among them. I kept on my tiptoes to look as tall as possible. The soldiers then began pulling out men from that group. I watched as one by one they were told to stand aside. Then, to my horror, they pointed to my father. He left the group and joined those who had been selected.

I tried not to cry or call out as I continued to push my body high into the air. My father turned and gave me one last glance. He quickly averted his gaze so not to call attention to me. Then his back was to me, and he was walking toward the group bound for the train station. I could not see his face as he marched away. I watched the very familiar hat he wore disappear around the street corner. That was the last time I would see him.

ARRANGING A DANGEROUS ESCAPE PLAN
OCTOBER 1942

The sight of my father's back as he walked away from me and toward the train station is indelibly imprinted on my mind. At the time, I still held out hope that maybe I would see him again soon. I did not know where they were taking him. I knew that it was probably to a death camp like Treblinka. And I never found out where he went. I suppose it does not matter, but I cannot help thinking about it and wonder. When a person loses a loved one, psychologists talk about them needing "closure." The more details they know about the fate of those loved ones, the easier it becomes to deal with the loss. For me though, I do not want to know, especially if it was a horrible death in one of those killing factories.

Once again, I found myself alone. That morning they had taken a couple hundred people away with my father. They were ramping up the effort to make Częstochowa "Judenrein." A few days later, they took us from the theater and put us in a newly formed ghetto. It was much smaller than the one before and there were only a few thousand of us left. Once here, they made us clean out the houses from the previous ghetto. They made us gather all the belongings that had been left behind as Jews fled or were captured during the vicious aktion from which I fled. We collected pots and pans, bedding and pillows, lamps, tables, chairs, everything that was not broken or destroyed. And we brought them back for the Germans and Poles to use.

Sometimes people tried to keep a few items for their own use or to try and use for barter. It was very dangerous to do so. Every evening, we were searched to see what we had. I remember a man was shot on the spot for trying to keep a sheet. I resolved not to take that risk, but soon I was put in a situation I could not resist—no matter the danger. These searches were often very thorough, almost complete body searches. But usually, they were only spot searches and not everyone was made to go through it.

By a stroke of luck, I was in a group that went to clean out the house where we lived just before the aktion. I couldn't believe it when we arrived there. Almost everything I had seen that night was still strewn around the house. I said nothing to anyone that this was my house. As I went through the rooms, I was delighted to find some of our photos. I stashed some of them in my shoe, others in my blouse, and some in my pants. When we returned to the ghetto that evening the usual searches were started. I held my breath hoping and praying that I would not be one of them. My heart raced frantically as they called out one after another to be examined. To my great relief, I was passed over and escaped punishment for taking the photos. I was so happy to have these. They were more valuable than gold to me at that point. It was my identity, my memories of those I loved most and my only connection to the wonderful life I had lived before the war.

A few days passed and I was given a new work assignment. They sent me to a nearby ammunition factory. The first few days, I worked in the kitchen peeling potatoes. It was not long before they moved me onto the factory line that made bullets. I don't remember much about the work, except that I operated a kind of press that stamped some identification on the casings of the bullets. The conditions continued to get worse over the next days and weeks. I had no way to keep clean. I was covered in lice and fearful that I would soon contract typhus. Those who operated the plant did everything they could do to humiliate and dehumanize us. The work was not strenuous, but it was stressful and painful nonetheless.

I began to think I would lose my mind very quickly in these conditions and wanted to run away. I remembered how difficult it had been on the run, trying to find hiding places and worrying if those I met along the way would help me, turn me in, or kill me on the spot. I could not think of doing that again. Another idea soon came to me.

I had heard stories of Jews being successfully smuggled out if they could get forged identification. With this identification and with the help of some Polish people, it was possible to blend into Polish society or at least go to an area that was safer. But this help did not come without a price and usually a very steep one. Where would I get the money or valuables to make such a transaction? Then I remembered Ms. Sporna who ran the grocery store and how she had helped me to escape just after the aktion. My mother had given her furs to this woman to keep when the Germans confiscated valuables from the Jewish people. The woman had agreed to keep them for my mother and return them at some point if it became safe to do so. The furs could be used to purchase my escape. There were so many obstacles to overcome to make this happen.

I knew the odds of my passing myself off for a long time as a Pole would be very thin and dangerous. Yet, if I could get away to the city where my mother's relatives lived, perhaps I would have better odds of surviving this madness. Będzin was my mother's hometown, and it was not too far away from Częstochowa. It had been annexed by the Germans at the start of the war, which meant that it was no longer in Poland. There would be a border that would have to be crossed, which would present great danger for me, but I was resolved to make this happen—or die trying. I simply could not take being alone anymore, especially in these conditions.

I am amazed at my ingenuity when I think back on this plan. I was only 12 years old. How could I accomplish the intricate steps necessary to make it happen? First, I had to get the furs from our Polish friend, but I would not be able to go there. I would have to get help from someone. Even under these strict conditions imposed in the new ghetto, there were some Jewish people who had a bit more freedom of movement. This was because of the work they had been assigned or their responsibilities with the Judenrat. How could I find such a person without risking revealing my plan to the wrong person?

Then one day came a stroke of luck. At mealtime, we were given a few loaves of bread. One of the men nearby handed me a loaf and a knife and told me to cut the bread so it could be divided. I stared at the bread and back at him. He realized that I did not know how to cut the bread. He took the loaf and the knife back and said, "Watch me. Like this," and began to cut it into even pieces. He laughed at me and struck up a conversation. His last name I remember was Jungerman. In a short while, he had told me enough about himself that I realized he was one of those people with connections and could be the one to help me get the furs. I told him about them, and he agreed to help. He would arrange to get the furs back and sell them in exchange for the forged papers and getting me across the border.

It seems so impossible to me when I look back on it. Again, a 12-year-old girl, arranging such a plot? But the task was made easier by the lure of money. There were people around who were desperate enough to take great risk to get it. In fact, the black market thrived in these topsy-turvy times. So perhaps it was not so unusual to get this help so quickly.

While getting the forged papers and having someone escort me to the border was the biggest task, there were other obstacles that had to be overcome. How could I get away from my work detail unnoticed? How would I link up with the smugglers at just the right time? So many things could go wrong with my daring plan. Despite so many uncertainties, I remained determined and carefully kept seeking help from those that could provide it.

In the meantime, I happened to meet my cousin who had survived the deportations to the death camps and was working in a nearby camp. Though it was a great surprise and joy to see her again, it was also a stroke of luck. She told me about a bunker in the ghetto where some other of my family members had been hiding. She told me that they would take me in for a few days while I waited to be smuggled. This bunker would serve as a transition for me until the right time to meet the smugglers.

Around the same time, the man who had contacted the smugglers told me of the plan to get me to them. He and some other Jews worked in a house just outside the ghetto as tailors, furriers, and shoemakers. Since this house was outside the ghetto, the Polish smugglers could come there to take me away. It was the perfect meeting place. But the timing had to be perfect as well. In order to meet them at the right time, I would have to be ready to go at a moment's notice. How could I do that while I was working at the factory?

Everything was finally arranged except for day and time. I was feeling very nervous that they may send for me while I was at the factory or at a time when I could not get out of the ghetto. I decided it was time to go to the bunker my cousin had told me about. So, one morning very early before I was supposed to go to work, I crept away to the house with the bunker. I was relieved to see it was there and that the people hiding there let me come in. My aunt, my cousin's mother, was there, and we were so happy to see each other.

I told her of my plan and that I would only be there for a few days at the most.

I was good to my word because it was only a couple of days that word came to me that it was time to meet the smugglers. I got up early that morning and gathered up the only possession I cared to take with me—the photos I had taken from my house. I didn't have much to take anyway, but I concluded that traveling lighter would be safer. I left the bunker and met up with the Jewish men who worked at the house where I was supposed to meet my Polish escorts. I blended into their group, and we all made our way to the house.

When I arrived, I found out that there were two other people who were going to be smuggled out at the same time. One of them was a young boy who was also going to reunite with relatives in Będzin. It was comforting to know I would have a companion, but I also worried that the two of us together might arouse more suspicion. Either way, I had no choice in the matter. I waited nervously among the tailors and other craftsmen for the smugglers to come. Finally, they arrived and took the three of us to their house nearby. We hunkered down for a long, anxious night waiting for our dangerous escape the next morning.

I did not sleep a wink.

SMUGGLED TO BEDZIN
MARCH 1943

Finally the morning came that we were to be smuggled out of Częstochowa. The smugglers came into our room and quietly said it was time to go. It was still dark outside and eerily quiet. The night before they had given us some forged identity papers with alias Polish names. We were told to say the names over and over in our minds to get used to saying it as a first instinct if we were questioned. I practiced all night.

Then it was time to go. The only thing I had brought with me other than the clothes on my back were my family pictures, the most precious things I owned. One of the smugglers noticed the box I held with the photos inside. He asked me what was in the box. I told him and he said it could be dangerous to have them with me if we were stopped and questioned. I pleaded with him to let me take them and he quickly conceded. I am sure he could see the disappointment in my eyes realizing I might have to leave them behind. More likely, he didn't want to lose any more time discussing it. We needed to go quickly now before it got too late in the morning.

We quietly left the house. Just outside, a wagon waited for us. We crawled into the back and covered ourselves with blankets to stay out of sight. The driver cracked the reins and the wagon lurched forward. The steady rhythm of the horse's hooves clopping against the road was comforting. After a few minutes I began to feel sleepy, but the beating of my anxious heart pounded in my head and prevented me from dozing.

The border was only a few kilometers from the smuggler's house. So it was not long before we were at the crossing point. They had chosen a point outside of town in the countryside so we could cross secretly. We didn't dare try to cross at a checkpoint. Our Polish accomplices traveled separately in another wagon for their safety. To be caught helping Jews to escape meant the death penalty.

The wagon driver signaled the horse to halt, and we came to a gradual stop. The driver dismounted from the wagon and tapped us through the blankets to let us know it was time to get out. As I threw the blanket off, I could see that daylight was just beginning to break. The air was still, and everything was quiet. Far off in the distance a dog let out a couple of barks. I knew the barking was most likely not directed at us because it seemed so far away. Nonetheless, the sound jolted me. Would there be other dogs that might reveal our escape?

The driver escorted us into the nearby woods where we could see a well-worn path leading into the thick, dark forest. He pointed down it and told us the border was just a few hundred meters down the path. The trail would emerge from the forest on the other side. At that point we would come upon a road and another wagon would be waiting for us. We thanked him and started walking.

The light of day was quickly growing, but the forest shade gave me comfort that we would not be spotted—at least for now. In just a few minutes, we were at the road he had told us about. But no wagon was waiting! My heart raced with fear. The road was deserted, and everything was silent. What now?

In a few seconds we heard hoofbeats and the rolling wheels of a wagon. We ducked back into the woods to wait for it to appear, not knowing if it was our ride or someone who would turn us in. We listened closely and peered through the branches to try and catch a glimpse. The noise of its approach grew louder, and we could tell it was slowing. The driver pulled the horse and wagon to a stop right in front of the trail head. Now we could see the driver through the thick brush and trees. It was obvious to us that he was waiting for something and looking down the path into the forest in anticipation.

With much trepidation, we slowly emerged from the woods and out into the road. The man motioned us to come quickly. We rushed up to it and vaulted into the back. I searched my pockets to make sure I still had the forged papers, and I practiced my Polish name under my breath. A sense of relief came over me as the wagon shifted forward. This time we did not hide but sat upright in the wagon and tried to appear as if all was normal. I clutched the box of photos tightly to my chest and once again tried to calm myself with the rhythm of the wagon's motion. My heart raced and robbed me of calm.

Where to next, I wondered. We had been told that our journey's final leg to Będzin would be by train. So I expected that we would arrive at a station in a nearby town. The driver said nothing to us and kept his gaze straight ahead. In a little while we arrived in a small town. It was just starting to come alive with the day's activities. It did not take long before we were in front of the town's station. The driver stopped and helped us get off the wagon. He handed me and the other boy train tickets. I looked at them and they both said Będzin. The driver wished us a pleasant voyage and good luck, calling us by our Polish names. It was as if he was reminding us to be careful and begin to play the part of our new identities.

Walking into the station was frightening, but I knew I had to show no fear and display full confidence. It was a small station and was already getting busy as the train would be there soon. We found the schedule board and noted the correct platform for our journey. Quickly, we made our way out to the tracks and found a place to sit and wait. It was only a few minutes before the sound of the whistle echoed down the railway. The train slowly crept into the station and stopped. Soon, we were on board.

Once on the train, we all separated and found seats away from one another. We did not want to create any suspicion by being together. Our smuggler also boarded the train and found a place to sit away from us. It was only a couple of minutes before the train started to move once again, but it seemed like an eternity. We were on our way. It would be a few hours until we would arrive in Będzin. I tried to relax but found it very difficult. I practiced in my head the pronunciation of my name as I nervously watched for the train conductor, or worse, the police.

Thankfully, my fear of that confrontation never materialized. Such a great sense of relief as we pulled into the Będzin station without having ever been checked or approached by any authority. As the train slowed, I jumped up and made my way to the gangway and took my place in the queue to disembark. I looked around at the passengers waiting to get off the train yet being careful not to make any eye contact. None of them cared to look me in the eyes either.

Once on the platform, a new reality hit me. I knew that my family would no longer be in the part of town where they had lived before the war. I realized that, by now, any Jews that had not been sent away to death or work camps would have certainly been confined to a ghetto like we had been in Częstochowa. So, now I had to determine quickly where to find the ghetto. I could not wonder aimlessly through the city for too long or I would be captured.

I knew the area a bit but not in much detail. My uncle had lived near the train station before being sent to the ghetto, so I knew the area around it to some degree. I also had found out that the ghetto in Będzin was in a part of the city known as Komnianka. This was fortunate knowledge for me. It would be easy enough to ask anyone in the town where the ghetto was. However, that would not be wise? Asking a question like that might very well give me away. But I could ask directions to Komnianka. I found an older woman who had a kind face and discretely asked the way. She told me, seemingly without any suspicion.

I wandered out of the station and into the town's streets, trying to look as if I belonged and on my way to a definite location. I walked at a fast pace but not so fast as to draw attention to myself or to miss the landmarks the old woman had given me. It was late in the afternoon now and the shadows stretched long across the town. The sides streets were now completely in shade cast by the buildings that lined it. The darker streets gave me more comfort though they probably did not help conceal me at all.

Suddenly, I turned a corner and looked down the street in front of me. At the end of it was the edge of the ghetto. I knew it had to be because of its very poor condition. The buildings were in bad repair and dilapidated. Further down the street I could see people who were Jewish. I quickly made my way to the neighborhood and into the heart of the ghetto.

Before the war, my grandfather had been a prominent businessman in Będzin with a successful insurance company. I was confident that anyone there would know him or at least of him. I approached an older man and asked if he knew him. To my delight, he did and directed me to his house. Once there, I knocked, and a lady opened the door. I did not know this lady, but I told her who I was looking for and she motioned me to a room down the hall. The living conditions in this house were very bad. Several families occupied it and my grandfather and grandmother were in the room she pointed out to me.

I slowly opened the door to see them crowded inside the room. They both looked as if they had seen a ghost. Their faces went white, and my grandmother's hands shot up to cover her cheeks. She gasped. Then I noticed her gaze went past me and over my shoulder as if someone had come in behind me. I turned around to see what she was looking at. There was no one there. I looked back at her with a confused look. Then she said, "Is your mother with you?"

There was no need for me to answer. She already knew even before she asked the question. She began to weep and came to hug me. My grandfather stood by, silent, unable to utter a word. His face was one of shock and fear.

Their lives now in the ghetto teetered on the edge. At any moment the end could come. Aktionen came frequently as the Nazis pushed harder for Judenrein. Jews were captured and sent away to the death camps without any warning and for no reason. They struggled to get enough food for their frail bodies. Filth was overtaking everything since they had no ability to clean properly. Typhus and other diseases were spreading rapidly. Now they had another person to worry about. And on top of that, I had no papers. Papers were now always required for everyone in the ghetto. The forged papers I had been given to get out of Częstochowa would not work here. They were for a Polish girl, and they would be useless for a Jew in the ghetto.

REUNITED WITH MY GRANDPARENTS
MARCH 1943

I was somewhat of a "favorite" grandchild to my mother's parents. Since I was the only one who lived far away and could only visit once or twice a year, they always fawned over me and gave me special treatment. My grandmother was a vibrant woman with great energy and resolve. She spoke confidently and powerfully and seemed to always know what was right in any situation. My mother and I used to go on vacation with her every summer to the resorts in the mountains of southern Poland. We were with her on that last vacation just before the war started.

My grandfather was such a wonderful and kind man. I loved him very much and I knew he loved me. He never expressed the fear about my arrival, but as I learned more about the situation, it was clear to me that he was weighted down by it. And his fears about me would soon be realized.

Without any papers, I could not even leave the house because the authorities often checked people on the street, even in the ghetto, to see if they had proper identification. If one was found without the legal papers, they were most often sent away to Auschwitz, Dachau, or Buchenwald. So I was in a very precarious position.

One day I ventured out. I do not remember why. Perhaps to try and find some food or maybe just because I could not take being confined in the house any longer. Either way, it was a dangerous decision. While walking along the street not very far from our house, a Jewish policeman stopped me and asked for my papers. These police were part of the Judenrat, Jews who were forced by the Germans to manage the affairs of the Jews in the ghetto. When I could not produce any papers, the policeman took me away to his office and held me there. I thought it was the end for me. Soon, however, they let me go. My uncle who was influential with the Jews in Będzin had somehow arranged my release.

From then on, I had no choice but to stay in the house at all times, but even this would not be safe. They began to conduct regular checks of the households in the ghetto to verify paperwork. We became the target of one of these checks. One night, the Jewish police knocked on our door and demanded to be let in. It did not take them long to discover I was without the proper paperwork. It was very late at night, and we were all in bed. The policemen said that I must go with them to the station. I was terrified and figured this was it for me. Surely now, having been caught for the second time, I would be sent away to a concentration camp.

My grandfather was sitting up in bed and began to plead with them not to take me., telling them that he needed me to help him get around because he was an invalid. I thought he concocted this story in desperation. He was old and did not move around very fast, but he was no invalid. Then he pulled back the blanket he was sleeping under. He pointed to one of his legs. To my great surprise, it was only a stump. I had never known before this incident that he had been wearing a prosthesis for years. The realization shocked me.

The men looked at the leg and thought for a few seconds. They looked over at me and then back at my grandfather. They apologized to him saying they must take me regardless since I did not have the proper identification and authorization to be in the ghetto. My grandfather pleaded with them again to let me stay, but to no avail.

At the station, I waited in terror for my fate to be determined. I sat there for hours without any resolution or seeming attempt at one. I imagined that my time had finally come and that soon I would be off to a death camp. All the times I had been on the run on my own, I had concluded that I would rather be back with my family and suffer the fate of a death camp than to be all alone and searching for my next bit of food and a safe hiding place. In resignation, I was ready to accept that fate. At least, I had been able to see my grandparents one more time.

Then something amazing happened. The policeman came to me and said I was free to go. He warned me not to be caught again or the penalty would be final. I had no idea why I was being let go, but I didn't wait to ask any questions. I ran out of the station and back to my grandfather's house. Once there, he told me that my uncle had bribed the police to secure my release. I knew now that I was a burden to my beloved family and must find somewhere else to go. Where? How? There were not many alternatives left for Jews by this point. Except to die.

My grandfather and grandmother had risked much to take me in so unexpectedly. Twice I had been caught and twice my uncle had to bribe the police for my release. Still, my grandfather did not put any pressure on me to leave. They knew I had no alternatives. However, I was desperate to find one to relieve their fears of arousing the retribution of the German and Polish authorities. And I could no longer bear to suffer like a prisoner inside our small room day and night.

I was unable to secure any papers that would allow me to move about in the ghetto. Even my uncles with their influence could not get them for me. Aktionen continued to occur frequently and more and more of the Jews in Będzin were being killed or sent off to the camps. My grandfather and grandmother never left the house because they were old. Older people were captured immediately and sent away. By this time, almost everyone stayed inside in hiding, only venturing for the absolute necessities. It was clear that the plan to make the city Judenrein was accelerating. I knew time was running out for my family and me.

Most of my mother's family was still alive and had survived the brutal aktionen. But how much longer could they continue to do so? They seemed to be waiting for some kind of miracle. I was certain that there no miracle was coming. The thought of that reality turned over and over again in my mind. Anxiety gripped me. Then an idea came to me.

I had heard that there were work camps nearby where Jews were forced to make products for the war effort. This labor was desperately needed by the Germans as most able-bodied men and women were sent off to the war front. As a result, Jews in these camps were not targeted for extermination. The camps conditions were severe, but they were not extermination camps. These Jewish slaves were fed daily, albeit very poorly, to keep their strength for the work.

I enjoyed working. So, I reasoned that would not be a problem for me. Working had been a welcome diversion for me when I returned to Częstochowa after being on the run. Being confined to the house was making me stir crazy. I felt as if I was being suffocated. And, of course, the constant threat of another roundup loomed heavily on my mind. I resolved to find a way to get into one of the work camps.

When I went to tell my grandfather of my decision, I expected him to try and dissuade me. His response surprised me. He took a completely neutral position and told me that he could not tell me what to do. He said that I must do what I think is best for me. To me, this was a discrete way of saying that I should go.

The very next day I went to the Jewish police and told them I wanted to volunteer to work in a camp. I realized that I might be signing my own death warrant by going to the police. Already I had been arrested two times for being without papers. What would they do to me now? Regardless, I was desperate to get out of the isolation and lessen the burden on my grandparents.

I was fortunate on this day. Rather than arresting me, they accepted my request and assigned me to a nearby camp called Bolkenhain where they made fabric of all kinds for the war effort. There I would meet two wonderful friends without whom I would not have survived. They would be surprised at my decision to volunteer to work at the camp. But just two weeks after I went there, the Będzin ghetto was liquidated.

I never saw my grandparents again.

INTO THE CAMPS-BOLKENHAIN
SEPTEMBER 1943

Sometimes remembering is hard work, but that is when it is most important to be done. And unfortunately, memories conjured up with such pain and labor, are usually the most unpleasant. Yet, even during the most difficult times, there are some returning thoughts that warm the heart. Among my memories from enduring the greatest horror in human history, I remember Lili and Halinka, two beautiful friends who helped me survive.

As I entered the door of the work camp, fear and dread welled up inside my chest and my heart pounded. Inside were scores of young women and girls like me. Most were not yet women. They were still children. I was somewhere in between. With our childhoods robbed from us, we had been forced to grow up quickly. I was 13 by that time, and already had seen more horror and narrowly escaped death more times than most people would in their entire lives.

I surveyed the room. The faces were thin and their expressions hollow. There were no smiles. No laughter. No excited chatter in which teenage girls should be engaging. It was as if their humanity had been stripped from them. That was certainly what the

Germans had tried to do. They did not see us as human, and they did their best to take away all our dignity.

Yet, hidden deep inside these overworked bodies there remained the will to fight for their humanity. They formed friendships to encourage and help one another to survive. They clung to one another in small groups. I was fortunate that I would be a part of one of those groups.

As I settled into my bunk, two girls approached me. I did not know what to expect. I had been alone now for so long. One of them introduced herself. "Hello. I am Lili." She let me know that I would be sharing my bunk with her. I told them my name and then turned to the other girl. "Hi, I am Halinka," she said. "Where did you come from?"

"I am originally from Częstochowa, but I fled from there because my parents had been sent away to concentration camps. At least, that is what I think. I am not sure. So, I came to Będzin to find my grandparents."

"Did you find them?" Lili asked.

"Yes, they are still there in the ghetto."

Halinka asked, "And why are you here? Did the Germans force you to come to work here?"

"No, I volunteered."

My answer surprised them. "Really! Why? No one volunteers to come to a work camp," Lili blurted out.

"I had no papers, and it was getting too dangerous, since I had already been caught twice without them and probably would have been sent away to a camp had it not been for my uncle who was able to bribe my way out both times. It was dangerous for me and for my family. I couldn't leave our little room in the tiny apartment in the ghetto because of the fear of getting caught again. I was going crazy, and I was fearful that we would all be sent away to a death camp. The aktionen were becoming more and more frequent and Jews were being killed and taken away. So I decided to take my chance in a work camp. I figured my chances for survival might be better here."

My answer made sense to them, but they were still amazed that anyone would volunteer to be in a forced labor camp.

"We work 12 hours a day. It is hard, tedious work," Halinka warned me. "You may soon wish you were back in the tiny room!"

"What do you make here?" I asked Lili.

"We make fabric of all types. For clothes, blankets, even parachutes," she answered.

"What are the conditions like?"

"We work long hours of course, 12 hours every day, but from what I have heard of the other camps, it is not as bad as it could be. We are not given much food, but they are not starving us. And, except for working us very hard, they treat us well,"

Lili said.

Halinka added, "They need the labor to keep the war effort supplied. So, they keep us alive. Your decision may prove to be the right one, but it is exhausting, and they are not too concerned with our comfort."

I had come to really like my new acquaintances. We had a lot in common. The three of us were from very similar backgrounds. Lili was one year older than me and from the town of Auschwitz, where the infamous death camp had been constructed. Halinka was from Będzin and the same age as me. We shared the same middle-class lifestyle growing up. We had studied many of the same things in school and had similar interests.

We were also quite alike as far as our religious upbringing. They had both been in religious families but not Orthodox. Yet we each had Orthodox grandparents. I suppose this was a common situation for the Jewish generations of the mid-20th century. Our parents were eager to adapt to the modern western world, yet they were not quite as eager to discard their faiths completely as many succeeding generations of Jews have done. In fact, quite the opposite. Our parents loved the traditions of Judaism and kept them faithfully. The three of us now realized deeply the value of those now that we could no longer celebrate them. We made sure to talk about them with each other and, when possible, to do something a little different on Shabbat or a Holy Day.

We loved to tell each other stories and hear about each other's families. It was great solace and therapy for us to remember them and hope that someday we might be reunited. Even though by this time I was almost certain none of my family had survived. It took some time for us to discover, but Halinka and I, after several discussions about our extended families, were delighted to find out that we had some relatives in common. Her family had come from Silesia where my mother was from, and the connection originated there. After such a long time, I can no longer remember how exactly we were related.

When I told her about the holidays we would take at the resorts in southern Poland, Halinka told me her family did as well. Of course, we had never met on any of those, but we were often in the same area at the same time. We reminded ourselves of those beautiful, fun-filled summer days. We conjured up images of the food, closing our eyes as we did so to remember the wonderful smells of those meals. We talked about helping our mothers with the baking and cooking, especially when a Holy Day was nearing. We even fondly remembered the other chores we were made to do for the family. We laughed about how much we hated doing them then, but how happy we would be to have them forced upon us once again.

The bonds among the three of us continued to grow stronger every day as we vowed to help each other. We were careful to help all the other girls in the camp if we could, but Lili, Halinka and I became extremely close. They were now my family, my sisters.

Little did I know at the time the horror we would soon experience together.

ON TO LANDESHUT
MARCH 1944

The Bolkenhain camp with its 150 female prisoners was relatively small compared to most other camps. After six months I had come to know them all to some degree. But Lili, Halinka, and I spent most of our time together. Lili and I shared the bottom bed of a bunk and Halinka was in the bed above us with another girl. I wish I could remember her bunkmate's name. She was also a good friend, but we never developed the fast bond with her that we had among the three of us.

We were best of friends and inseparable. Sadly, that would come to an end. The camp at Bolkenhain was going to be converted to a munitions factory. It was announced that we would all be transported to other camps. Where would we be sent, and would we still be together?

A few days later, we were put on trains bound for our new work camps. I was so relieved that Lili and I were put on the same train. We would be sent to a camp called Landeshut, which also was a weaving and fabric factory. To our great disappointment, Halinka was put on a train to another camp, but did not know where she was going. We were so fearful that we would never see her again. We worried for her because she had always been the frailest of the three of us. How would she fare without her dear friends? How would we fare without her? Our "threefold cord" had been broken.

Our first few days at Landeshut were not too different from Bolkenhain. The work was similar: spinning thread and weaving fabric. We were supervised in our work by older German men who were too old to fight in the war but knew the trade of fabric making. Our guards and slave masters were of the German air force, or Wehrmacht, which ran this and many other labor camps. This was a more fortunate situation. The feared Nazi SS ran the concentration and death camps, and they were much crueler. At that time, the SS had very little to do with the labor camps that were established to support the war effort rather than to eliminate Jews. We were basically slave labor and barely kept alive, but at least they wanted to keep us alive. As the war worsened for the Germans, that would change. And the SS would eventually take over the labor camps as well.

Now in Landeshut, I was beginning to feel that change starting. It was not as clean as Bolkenhain, and the food was meager. I was hungry all the time. And there was one big difference that I found difficult to get used to. We worked through the night. During the day, Germans staffed the factory. After their shift was over, we came to take over and work through the long nights. Each evening we were lined up in rows at the bunkhouse and marched to the factory. It wasn't very far so the marching was not rigorous. But it was another way to humiliate us. We had to keep in time while armed guards marched alongside to make sure we did so, and would return to our bunkhouse, once again marching in strict lines, just after the break of day.

I found it most difficult to sleep during the day, especially when it was hot and humid. Lili also struggled to sleep even though we both were always exhausted and sore from our work. We often spent the mornings talking until our eyes could no longer stay open. It was the only way to pass the time. However, we soon found another activity that would help us overcome the monotony.

Lili was very resourceful and creative. She was also a very good seamstress. She found ways to sneak away with thread and sewing needles from the factory floor. We were able to sew together a few pieces of clothing, the most practical of which were some underwear. We made other things to wear as well—kerchiefs, scarves, and decorative things. We made nothing very fancy although some of the things were very beautifully done. We could not have worn them anyway because it would have brought unwanted and dangerous attention to us. And our sewing activities would have been over—or worse, perhaps our lives. So, at first, it seemed our efforts were totally impractical. And indeed, they were. But the most important thing about it was we had something to do, an activity that could divert our minds from the hard work and terrible conditions. More importantly, it helped to remind us that we were still human.

However, we soon found something more useful for our risky pastime. Some Jewish women were assigned to act as go-betweens for us and the administrators of the camp. They were older women and were called *Judenältesten*. They had privileges for performing this service, but they were often put in difficult positions as they walked the line between doing their duty and protecting their fellow Jews. We had learned that they were not above bribery. With that knowledge, we began to use our needlework to curry favor with them. We exchanged these for bits of extra bread or more soup.

The Germans tried their best to dehumanize us. The lack of food, the poor living conditions, and the attitude of superiority they subjected us to were all designed to break us. They expected us to behave like animals under these conditions because that is what they thought of us. We knew they could take away our health or even our lives, but we were not going to let them take away our dignity. Here at Landeshut we had been successful in this fight. But soon we would get the news we were being moved to a new camp and Landeshut would be shut down or transformed into another type of factory. We would no longer be needed here. We were on our way to Grünberg, a much larger factory with a sadist commandant. Would we be able to keep our dignity there?

MOVED AGAIN-GRÜNBERG CAMP
JULY 1944

Lili and I huddled close together as we were marched into the new labor camp. The building was very large and imposing on the city streets of Grünberg. We walked through the large door leading into the bunks. Rows and rows of closely crowded bunks awaited us. There was barely enough room for us to squeeze through to our newly assigned beds. Once again, Lili and I would share a bunk.

Already we could sense the more severe conditions of this camp. Firstly, it was so much bigger. By now there were over 1,000 women and more would come, actually hundreds more than in Landeshut. We could see the women here were more gaunt and more tired. This factory was also engaged in making fabric, but in a much more extensive process since it was involved in the entire process, from the creation of yarn and thread, all the way to the weaving and bolting of the fabric.

Very soon after we arrived, other woman began to arrive from small camps around Silesia. A new hall had been opened for these new arrivals, and it was a large warehouse with a very high ceiling. This factory was a horror for all of us, but paradoxically, it was a beautiful building with stunning gardens and landscaping all around. When we arrived, it was late spring of 1944 when flowers of all kinds were blooming magnificently everywhere on the grounds. It was the only sight for us that brought joy.

But it would not be long before we saw another joyful sight: Halinka arrived! She told us that she had been sent to a camp in Merzdorf. Conditions there were bad like those in Landeshut. She told us that there were about 100 women there and that they also made fabric like in Bolkenhain, but they were occasionally forced to do harder labor such as brick laying and unloading coal to fuel the factory. Another difference at Merzdorf was that the prisoners were loaned out to local businesses for all types of work. Every day, men would come to the camp and select women to work for them. She told us it was like a slave market.

We were very happy that the three of us were together again, but what awaited us would deprive us of any happiness.

Daily life at Grünberg would be much worse for us than in Landeshut. Yet we were much better off than other camps, especially the concentration camps. They did not shave our heads and they allowed us to keep relatively clean. We were allowed to bathe every two weeks. We could wash our clothes and bedding. At least we had bedding which in other camps they did not. We had pillows and blankets here and slept on sacks of straw rather than directly on hard wooden bunks. There was no attempt to work us to death because they desperately needed the labor. Even more so now because the war was turning on them. Not until we arrived here did we begin to sense that change.

Soon our food rations were cut back and the length of time for lights to be on in the bunkhouse shortened. After the weather turned colder, the buildings were often not heated. We were beginning to feel the consequences of the Germans beginning to lose the war.

Because there were so many women at Grünberg, we faced other hardships that we did not face in the smaller camp of Landeshut. We had to endure morning and evening roll calls. With over 1,000 people to count these were excruciatingly long and arduous. We stood outside in rows of five. We were forced to remain completely silent and still while our numbers were called out one by one. When we first arrived, it was summer. The heat and humidity that year was unusually extreme. When winter came, we were forced to be on roll call very early in the morning, no matter the weather. Often, we stood in freezing rain, wind, and snow. It seemed that these roll calls started earlier and earlier as the winter months progressed. For one of them, we were woken up at 3:30 in the morning. If the count was not correct, it would start all over. Sometimes, it could take a couple of hours to complete.

The food was inferior to Landeshut from the very beginning. We would get one tiny piece of bread in the morning and had to last us the entire day. Occasionally we were given a bowl of soup. It was mostly water with a trace of some vegetables, but the warmth of it was welcomed.

Things continued to worsen. The biggest threat was tuberculosis. The camp had had an outbreak of it before we arrived and new cases were continuing to appear. Every few weeks we were x-rayed to see if we had developed the deadly lung disease. If the exam showed black spots on one's lungs, they were immediately sent away. Usually this would be to a death camp, and from here the closest one was the dreaded Auschwitz. When it was time for these examinations, fear gripped us all. Fortunately, I never showed signs of contracting it.

Despite the worsening conditions, we did our best to maintain our dignity. It was important for us to look as pretty as we possibly could, even though our surroundings were squalid. I remember putting curls in my hair with curlers made from rags to create a hairdo. It was a poor attempt at a "pageboy" style, which was a straighter hair style than a curly or wavy one. In this style the curls were at the bottom of the hair and tucked under. The pageboy was very much in fashion before the war. I still had a few clothes that were in decent condition. None of us had many clothes so we shared with each other, trading outfits so we could have some variety. I remember I had an outfit that was like a jumpsuit. I used to sleep on it in a way that would keep it creased.

Even with our efforts, we still looked quite pitiful. We were very skinny, and the clothes were mostly dirty and tattered. But we did not look like the prisoners so famously photographed from the other camps like Buchenwald and Auschwitz. All this effort allowed us to maintain our humanity. Sometimes it seemed so futile. Looking back on it now, I am convinced this was key in keeping our hopes alive and preparing us to endure the terror which was about to come.

THE SS TAKE OVER
OCTOBER 1944

Sometime in the autumn of 1944, the operation of the Grünberg camp changed. The SS took control of the camp and replaced the Wehrmacht. One day soon after, a truck rolled the courtyard of the camp and dozens of women, dressed in SS uniforms jumped out of the back. A little while later, a group of male SS guards also arrived. It was clear that they were now in charge. For the first time we felt as if our lives were in danger.

The new commandant of Grünberg enjoyed every excuse to inflict physical pain on the girls. Many times, with no cause or reason, he would strike one of us. Sometimes he would say it was for talking too loud or too much. But he was sadistic, and that was the only reason he needed. He wore a large ring on his finger with the "*Totenkopf*" design on it. This was the infamous Nazi symbol featuring skull and crossbones. It was a primary symbol for the SS throughout the war. Just before the commandant would strike one of the girls, he would twist the ring around on his finger so the head with the symbol was in his palm. The hard metal of the ring would cut deep into the face or head of his target.

Prior to the arrival of the SS, we had only worked six days a week and were given Sundays off. After the changeover, the new commandant often used Sundays to rob of us this time to recuperate by calling a roll call and making us stand in formation for hours. At the end, he delivered a lecture telling us we would be kept alive as long as we produced. He was also very eager to tell us that the only way we would ever see freedom would be through the smokestacks.

One day after our new guards arrived, some girls in the camp were coming back from the factory through the courtyard. Suddenly, a piece of bread sailed over the wall from outside the camp. One of the girls ran to it and grabbed it. Just then, an SS guard caught sight of her and called out for them to stop. He made them stand still while he asked them about the bread. One by one, each girl bravely denied knowing where the bread came from even though some of them did know. And one by one, after each denial, the guard beat the girls, bloodying their faces, necks, and heads. Despite the painful blows, the girls supported each other and did not give into his cruelty. The male SS guards were cruel, but in many ways the female guards were even crueler. When the women guards marched us, they often accused of us of not marching fast enough. When they did, they punched us with their rifle butts while they shouted loudly at us.

One day, we were rounded up by the woman guards and marched to a nearby building. This was another time when they shouted at us and beat us as we marched. One by one we were called inside the building to a room where several men sat in white coats. On the floor in front of them, a white circle had been drawn. As we entered the room, we were forced to strip completely naked. Then we were told to stand in the middle of the circle. The men appeared to be doctors, but none of us thought they were. All around the rest of the room stood SS soldiers, both men and women. I noticed that their faces were very young for soldiers. I did not know why at the time, but looking back, this was a sign of the end of the war for them. Their forces had been so depleted, that they were turning to the youth, sometimes children, to serve on the home front as guards.

They said nothing to us but only stared at us in silence. They remained emotionless and made no effort to examine us in any way. They took no notes, nor did they discuss with each other the reason for this strange inspection. Fortunately, they did not touch us either, but for several minutes they gazed at us in the most humiliating way. Then we were given a necklace to wear with a number attached to it. The number served a similar purpose as those tattooed on the victims of Auschwitz. We were glad we were not tattooed, but this had been almost as humiliating. We concluded afterwards that this was purely an exercise to further dehumanize us. It was a psychological ploy to break us further down into submission to their belief of being a superior race. And we also thought that it was also some kind of perverted way of deriving pleasure. A sick and twisted "sex show" perhaps? Superior race indeed!

There had been times in the other camps that we had been a target for such humiliating and dehumanizing tactics, but now it was more frequent. The guards who had replaced the Wehrmacht guards were much more derisive of us all. They took every opportunity to shout at us and to degrade us with words and actions. We knew now that this was no longer a labor camp but had become a concentration camp. Work would still be done to make the fabric, so needed for to continue the war effort, but the new purpose would ultimately be to eliminate us.

This event was very frightening and after that, our work schedules and daily routines became more and more erratic and uncertain. When we had a more regular routine, without these strange inspections, we felt more secure. But that comfort had been replaced by a deep-seated fear of what would come next.

From that point forward, the daily roll calls became more erratic as well. We were woken up at different times of the morning. We were forced to wait longer once called into formation for the roll calls before the tallying would begin. It was now late November or early December, and cold weather was increasing. Just as that summer had been hotter than usual, the winter of 1944-45 would be excruciatingly cold. As long as we were at the camp and had the bunkhouse to retreat to, we could survive that.

THE MARCH BEGINS
DECEMBER 1944

Sometime in late 1944, the majority of the male SS guards left Grünberg leaving mostly female guards to watch over us. I can deduce now that they were probably sent to the Eastern Front to fight the Soviet army. While at the camps, we had no way to know what was happening in the war. The only time the officials in the labor camps told us anything was to announce some victory by their forces. This was an attempt to discourage us. But these reports were given less frequently over the past few months.

One day in December, we awoke to see heavy snow falling. It was beautiful as it covered the grounds and sculpted shapes of white along the trees and shrubs surrounding the buildings. For us it was not a welcome sight. We were already so cold, and they were no longer heating the buildings. I shivered wondering what would happen to us next. Our work schedule had become inconsistent, and we had not been examined or x-rayed in a long time. Something was changing for the Germans. Would that bring us good news or bad news?

Suddenly, an air raid siren blasted over the city. The guards began to panic and quickly scurried to their bomb shelters. We were told to stay inside the factory, but the machines were not running, and the power had been turned off. Here we sat, waiting for bombs to drop. We knew that if they did, the factory would be the prime target. We were sitting ducks for the Soviet bombers. It struck fear in my heart but, strangely, the sound of those sirens brought hope and joy. We thought that the Russians might be winning and getting close. To be so far into the German territory meant they had them on the run. Perhaps the war would be over soon.

As the next few weeks passed, the air raid sirens became more frequent, which raised our hopes even more, though we knew a bombing could be the end of us too. Most of the work had ceased. Not completely, of course, but enough for us to realize that the Germans were not faring well. By January 1945, the sirens sounded almost every day. At times, we could hear bombs falling and exploding in the distance. We were glad they were far away, and we assumed that this factory would have to be on the target list for the Russians.

It seemed that every day the guards' hatred toward us increased since they verbally abused us and beat us more often. The roll calls were longer and crueler as they made us stand for hours outside in the cold. These SS guards were so intimidating and frightening. Their black uniforms caused chills running up my spine. I tried my best to stay as far away from them as possible. It was always a relief when we were back in our bunks, and they were out of sight.

Then one day, there was no roll call. We were not marched to the factory. We waited for a long time expecting to be told to come out to be counted. A few nervous hours passed. Suddenly, a group of guards came into our bunkhouse and demanded that we gather all our belongings and prepare to leave. Where were they taking us?

They sent us to another bunkhouse where the women prisoners lived who had arrived before us. We pushed our way into the overcrowded space. There were not enough bunks for all of us. Lili, Halinka and I found a place to sit on the floor and waited. What would come next? How could we all live in such crowded conditions?

Soon we heard other prisoners coming into the camp. Later we learned that these were Hungarian-Jewish women who had been marched here from another camp in the East. These women were put in the bunkhouse we had just vacated. We looked out to get a glimpse of them. They were so thin and gaunt. Some of them had visible blood stains on their clothes and feet. Their heads were shaved and their faces pale and shrunken. Some of them had wooden clogs as shoes while others had no shoes at all. Those who were shoeless had wrapped their feet in rags to give some protection. There were hundreds of them. I do not know exactly how many, perhaps 500, maybe even 1,000.

They filled the bunkhouse, and we could hear them through the walls as they took over the space. There was a lot of commotion. Shrieks and cries echoed against the walls. Bunks and tables being turned over and crashing to the floor. The women were ransacking everything desperately looking for bits of food, pieces of clothing, or anything else that might be of the least value. It was a frightening sound.

The Hungarian Jews had suffered greatly after German invaded the country in 1941. Although Hungary was allied with Germany at that time, Hitler feared that the prime minister was secretly planning to switch allegiance and ally with Britain, Russia, and the US. The prime minister had allowed Jews fleeing from Poland to enter Hungary and refused to expel them. So, when the Nazis took over in 1941, the Jews were treated very badly. In Poland, the Germans took a slower approach to the disenfranchisement and eventual killing of Jews. But in Hungary, it was much faster paced.

Many of the Hungarian Jews were immediately expelled and sent to Poland and other Eastern European countries. Families were split up during these expulsions and they were sent to some of the harshest labor camps. So, these women had suffered more than we. They seemed to have given in more to the dehumanization tactics of the Nazis. We would find it difficult to socialize with them, not only because of their emotional and mental state, but also because most all of them spoke only Hungarian.

We learned that these women had come from Schlesiersee, a camp southeast of Grünberg. They had been marching for eight days and almost 100 kilometers in bitter cold. At the beginning of the march, they had each been given a loaf of bread that was supposed to last for the entire march. Because these women did not know where they were going or how long the march would take, many of them ate the bread too fast and were without food for most of the trek. No wonder they were so exhausted and desperate. Along the way some of the women were murdered. At about the halfway mark between the two camps, 40 women who became too weak to continue walking, were taken into a forest, and were gunned down. They were buried in a mass grave nearby.

We waited and listened as gradually the commotion in the next building died down. We wondered why they had been brought here to join us. The work in the factory had almost ceased so why bring in more slaves to work there? It did not make any sense. As the next day passed, we sensed the tension and nervousness among the guards growing. We all realized that the war was going badly for the Germans. We knew the Soviets were close because of the continuous sound of air raid sirens and bombs in the distance. We were encouraged by that reality, yet at the same time, we believed that these murderers would not want us to survive to tell our stories.

Two days after the Hungarian women arrived, the guards came to our bunkhouse and ordered us outside with all our belongings. As we filed outside into the snow-covered courtyard, the Hungarian women came out and were lined up beside us. The courtyard continued to fill from the buildings. Soon over 2,000 women and girls were stood in tight lines. The guards pushed and shoved girls to force them closer together and to stand in straight lines. Those who did not move fast enough were slapped or punched.

Fear gripped us since we were not told what was happening. Quiet sobbing and weeping interspersed the ranks, but most everyone kept silent and did not say a word. We waited for instructions or an announcement that would reveal their plan.

Then the gates of the courtyard opened. The guards began to separate the women into two groups. As they split the two columns, the girls were brutally shoved and pushed apart. Some women at the column divide were separated from their friends. They tried to move from one group to the other, but the guards began to hit and slap them and forced them back. Fortunately, Lili, Halinka, and I were not at the dividing point, so we remained together.

Once the two groups were separated, we were ordered to start marching through the camp gates. The Hungarian women came from a camp that had fallen behind the Soviet lines. The Germans marched them to our camp so that could not be liberated or tell the story of the horrors they had seen. Now we were to join them. For many weeks, we believed that Grünberg would fall under Russian control soon. As that reality came, our hopes also rose that maybe we would be liberated.

As we marched through the gates, our hearts sank; they were taking us with them as they evacuated. They were not going to leave us behind to tell their murderous story.

Lili, Halinka, and I grabbed each other's hands as we took the first steps out into the frozen snow. Where were we going? How long would it take? Would we survive? No one knew. Not even our captors.

As Lili, Halinka, and I moved forward and through the gates of the weaving factory, I looked around at all the girls beginning the march. There were 2,000 of us in total, divided into two groups of about 1,000 each. Once out and into the street, they began marching the groups in opposite directions. Our group was heading to the southwest and the other group was moving northwest. We had learned from Hungarian women about their terrible ordeal marching to Grünberg. Now we knew we were going to have to endure the same. They had marched for eight days without enough food, proper shoes, or clothing. How long would we march? And how would we be treated? Had I known the answers to those questions when we started the march, I do not think I could have continued to walk. It would have been too much to bear. For now, I could only have hope that I could last a few days like the Hungarian women on their march. If these girls had survived it, then perhaps I could as well. Their march lasted eight days. The days for us would be weeks.

INTO THE COLD-FROM GRÜNBERG TO BAUTZEN
JANUARY 1945

I lost track of time. I did not know the date or even the day of the week when we set out on the march, but knowledge of the history of the march revealed that we left Grünberg on January 29, 1945.

Before we started marching, we were given a thin blanket, a bowl, and a spoon. Then they gave each of us a partial loaf of bread and a little bit of sugar. We did not have the proper clothing for the brutal cold and wet snow but most of us had more than one set of clothes. Rather than carry the clothes in our arms, we put everything we had on in layers to help minimize the cold. Most of us had shoes. I still had my wooden clogs given to me by Ms. Sporza. Many of the women did not have shoes so wrapped their feet in rags.

The first day we marched 30 kilometers. Along the way, the guards were eager to instill fear in us. They made sure we knew any attempt at escape was futile and would mean instant death. Delays would not be tolerated.

Not long into the march one of the girls collapsed. Her friends tried desperately to help her up and continue. One of the guards turned, walked up to the girl on the ground, and shot her point blank in the head. Her friends screamed and cried as the guard shouted for them to keep moving or they too would be shot. We continued to march, and the guards left the girl's body lying in the street.

A little while later, another girl stopped to scoop up some snow to quench her thirst. Before she could put it into her mouth, a guard came from behind and clubbed her over the head with his rifle butt. She fell to the ground. Then he kicked her as he shouted for her to get up and keep marching. The girl jumped up quickly before the guard could shoot her.

In a couple of days, we reached the town of Christianstadt which had a labor camp serving as a munitions factory. We stayed at the camp through the next day and were not forced to march. The rest was very welcome, but our fears were not allayed.

During the night, a few dozen women escaped. Later the next day, most of them were brought back. They had been badly beaten. Those that did not return had been shot. The message from these beatings and killings was clear for my two friends and me—trying to escape was futile. Even if we were successful, where would we go? I knew the fear and uncertainty of being on the run with no permanent place to hide. I had been very lucky to survive my time on the run. But I knew that eventually luck would run out. And if we failed in an escape, it would most likely mean a brutal beating or a bullet in the head. We would see many of those in the coming weeks.

We knew that continuing to march in our pitiful condition and the lack of food and clothing was just as dangerous. So, Lili, Halinka, and I could not help but think about escaping. Every time we stopped, we surveyed the area and thought hard about how we might be able to get away at that moment. We looked for any place nearby to hide behind, under, or inside. We calculated our chances of going undetected while the others marched on. We knew the Russians were close behind. Perhaps, if we ran away, we could find them, and they would protect us. But no opportunity arose that we were brave enough to try.

We stayed two nights at Christianstadt. On February 2, we began again. Some women from the labor camp were forced to join the march. Over the next few days there were several escape attempts. All of them ended with the girls being shot. Many of them were beaten badly before being killed.

A few days after leaving Christianstadt, the march was unexpectedly halted. We were told to stand at attention. We heard cries and screams from a nearby forest while several SS guards emerged from the trees dragging a group of women who had tried to escape. The women were begging for mercy, but their pleas would not be heard. They brought them out and lined them up in front of us.

The commandant of the march approached the women. I learned after the war that the commandant's name was Karl Herman Jäschke. Jäschke was an SS officer who had worked at Auschwitz. He was especially cruel and sadistic. He was tried and convicted after the war for his crimes.

Jäschke approached the girls and pulled out his pistol. One by one he shot them in the head as they cried and pleaded for their lives. His face remained completely emotionless as he killed all 14 of the girls. They did not have to say anything more to us at that point. The murders did all the warning necessary.

For the next few days there were no more attempts to escape. On February 7, we reached the town of Weisswasser. Already we had been on the march for 10 days. It had seemed like a month or more. We were so tired and cold. We never took our clothes off when it was time to sleep. It was always too cold. So we slept in them and they grew filthier day by day. Soon we were infested by lice. We all knew the danger of that—typhus. One more threat of death was upon us.

After a couple of days, we arrived in the town of Bautzen where we experienced one of the most frightening confrontations with these evil murderers.

THE EXECUTION AT BAUTZEN
FEBRUARY 1945

Time moves steadily, persistently, and consistently. We know that seconds, minutes, hours, and days are precisely measured. Humans have always studied the sun, moon, and stars and created calendars that do not fail to prepare us for the changes in seasons. There are circumstances that distort time. Events in our lives can disrupt the rigid division of past, present, and future. During the winter of 1945, time often seemed to slow almost to a full stop. At others, it raced past as fast as the howling winds that beat at us as we walked.

How many days had we been marching? I stopped counting long before we reached Bautzen. It did not matter anymore. I could only think about the present moment and how to survive it. However, the question of how many more days we would be forced to march was always on my mind. How long could I last in this hunger and cold?

Already, many girls had died or been killed. There would be many more that would meet the same fate. In fact, most of them. We were only fragile women and girls. The strongest of men would not have lasted any better, faced with these horrible conditions. It often snowed, with wind blowing forcefully and bitterly. We had very little food and our clothing was becoming threadbare. The nights were long and frightful. Almost every morning, we woke to see more girls had died as they slept.

Thankfully, most nights we slept in a barn or some other building that our captors commandeered to shelter us. One night, we slept in a bombed-out church. Of course, most of these buildings did little to protect us other than to block the winter winds. There was never any attempt to provide heat for us. Usually, we had no choice but to sleep pressed together tightly since the buildings were barely big enough to contain the hundreds of us. But this cramped situation helped keep us from freezing to death. Lili, Halinka, and I usually cuddled together for warmth.

A few of the Hungarian women in our ranks were treated differently. They never slept out in the cold, nor suffered as greatly from hunger. They had sold their souls and the SS guards who bought them had female company in return. We resented them and could not understand how they could do such a thing. But looking back, I am not so critical. In desperate times, desperation easily sets in, and survival instincts take over. Like those Jews who served in the Judenrat, the organizations set up in every city, town, and village across Poland by the Nazis to help them deal with the Jews. Some of those in the Judenrat did their best to mitigate the cruel treatment of their communities. But there were many stories of those who took advantage of their position for more than just their own survival. Some were corrupt and sought financial gain. However, most of these became victims as well and it is this short sightedness that deserves the most criticism rather than their greed or desire for self-preservation.

Many of the girls lost the instinct for self-preservation. I remember seeing some of them sitting down in exhaustion or falling to their knees from hunger and weakness. Others' feet were frost bitten or so bloodied that the pain halted them regardless of their desire to continue. When this happened, their fates were sealed. I couldn't look back when I heard the gunshots ringing out to kill those who stopped. It was a daily occurrence.

Sometimes girls would attempt to run away or hide. When they were found missing, we were all stopped while the guards shouted at us to reveal where they had gone. Usually no one answered, mostly because no one knew. This angered them even more. Sometimes in these instances, they would select a girl randomly and then beat her severely or shoot her.

The thought of running away continued to occur to Lili, Halinka, and me. The Soviet army was close behind us. We could hear fighting and bombing in the distance. We saw German and Polish people fleeing the frontlines and the battles. We spoke German and Polish well enough to feel that we might be able to blend in with them pretending to be refugees. But the fear and dread of being on the run persisted for me. I still believed from my previous experience that we would most likely be discovered. For now, we determined the safest place was to stay in the ranks, do what we were told and try our best not to draw attention to ourselves. Yet, the idea of getting away from this hell as soon as we could was too alluring. At every stop, we looked for potential places to hide or run away.

That night in Bautzen, we slept in a large empty warehouse. In the morning we were called out of the building and into the courtyard. To our amazement, there was a large wagon filled with loaves of bread. We lined up in several rows and marched past the wagon where we were each given one whole loaf. We were surprised but happy that they were giving us so much bread at one time. Our delight would not last long.

Once back in the building, the guards started shouting for us to return to the courtyard. We were forced into rows of five and there was a roll call. Afterwards, Jäschke appeared in front of us. He said that there were some loaves of bread missing and demanded to know who had taken more than their share. No one answered. He continued shouting and threatened to keep us standing outside all night unless someone told him what happened to the loaves. Despite this, all the girls remained silent. Jäschke grew ever more enraged. His solution to satisfy his anger and get the information he wanted would shock and terrify us.

Jäschke instructed the guards to count off every 10th person. Each of them was taken from the ranks and they were gathered in a separate group. Several guards surrounded them and began to march them to a nearby wood. After they disappeared, some more guards came and selected a few girls to follow them. One of them was my friend Lili. I was terrified for her. We locked eyes as she was pulled away toward the woods. She said nothing to me nor I to her, but our expressions acknowledged this might be the last time we would see each other.

The girls were now out of sight. We all stood motionless and silent in the cold air. The pain of waiting in this uncertainty made it colder. Suddenly, we heard gunshots from the woods. With each pop I shuddered. My dear Lili, I thought. Have I lost you? Please, please come back.

Finally, the shots stopped. We waited in line. No one spoke. The only sound was that of sobbing trying to be held back. Eventually, we were allowed to return to the building. I tried to come to grips with the fact that Lili was gone. Halinka and I sat close together but we did not speak.

Hours went by and night finally came. We were convinced now that Lili was dead. But a miracle happened. We looked up and saw Lili coming toward us. She had two loaves of bread in her hands and sat down beside us. She divided one of the loaves into three parts and gave us each one of them. Though traumatized, Lili found a way to tell us what happened. The first girls selected were shot in cold blood. The second group of girls were taken to undress the murdered girls and bury them. For her work, Lili was rewarded with an extra loaf of bread. We ate the bread slowly, but we had been so hungry for so long it the extra pieces were devoured too quickly. We did not express any emotion as we ate, but I could not help but think that we were eating "blood bread."

ON A BRIDGE IN DRESDEN
FEBRUARY 1945

The "blood bread" filled our stomachs, but it did not satisfy. Emotionally we were starving as well. The three of us could not speak of the mass execution in the forest. I don't know how many girls had been shot. Probably dozens. I thought about how easily I could have been one of them.

Guilt began to plague me. Why had I survived so many times when others did not? Just as quickly as the guilt came, envy replaced it. Perhaps it would have been better to have been chosen and taken into the forest and to have it end right then and there. They were the lucky ones. No more pain and misery for them. Having survived, today I am tremendously thankful that I was spared. But in the moment just hours after this brutal and evil act, it was easy to believe death was preferable over the pain of continuing to walk.

We choked the bread down. Lili shivered as she remembered the faces of the girls she was forced to undress, dig their graves, and bury them. We ate in eerie silence, our faces devoid of any emotion. We could no longer feel. We were beaten down. Our humanity was slowly being drained from us like blood from an open wound. They had taken everything from us—our livelihoods, our homes, and our families. Now they were taking our hearts and souls. The scene at Bautzen was permanently etched in our minds. But it would stay there imprisoned forever. We would not speak of it again.

The next day we were on the move again. It was the middle of February 1945, perhaps the 11th or 12th but I am not sure. I only know the approximate date now because of the momentous event we were going to witness in the next day or two. Along the road, we began to see signs indicating the direction and distance to the city of Dresden. Anyone who knows the history of World War II will know that February 13, 1945 was a dark day for that city.

Bautzen is about 65 kilometers from Dresden. The weather had turned milder, almost springlike. The respite from the bitter winter weather we had faced was welcomed. As we got to the outskirts, we could see smoke billowing up from the center of town. The beginning of the total destruction of Dresden had begun in the middle of the previous night. What we were about to witness when we got there would stun us all.

As we moved into the outskirts of the city, smoke and flames were everywhere. Buildings were in rubble. Twisted steel and concrete formed strange sculptures down the streets. Suddenly, air raid sirens began to blast from various directions. Soon after, we heard the humming of hundreds of airplanes. It grew louder and louder into a deafening roar as we entered the city. The sky was now completely blanketed by clouds. We could not see the planes, but their noise was deafening. Then we heard the whistling of bombs plummeting to the ground. Explosions began to ring out all around. The earth shook violently. Meanwhile, we had to continue marching.

Flames were now arching up into the city skyline. Buildings were crumbling right before our eyes. It was an eerie sight because the streets were completely empty since all the residents were sheltering. We marched through the empty streets to the center of the city. We came to one of the main bridges that crossed the Elbe. The SS guards forced us to march onto the bridge after which they retreated for shelter along the riverbank and waited. They knew that the bridges of the city would be a primary target and left us there hoping the bombs would finish their murderous task.

Perhaps they thought that if the bombs didn't kill us, we would be terrified to death. But quite the contrary. Spontaneously, every one of the girls began to cheer. The shout of glee surprised me. But I had felt the same and could not contain it. I was surprised that so many of my comrades felt it too. Such joy was ironic and irrational. Why did we feel it?

Surprisingly, it was not for vengeance. Although we could have been justified to see the destruction of a proud German city of the "Third Reich" and think, now they would know a small bit of the horror we had faced. For most of us this did not enter our minds. Instead, our cheers were from the thought that our ordeal might soon be over. And not because we thought it was the end of our captors. Our joy came because we hoped the bombs would strike us and put us out of our misery. A quick death would be preferred to the agonizing torture of this march.

We stood on the bridge for what seemed like hours but it may have only been a few minutes. The bombs continued to rain down with increasing intensity. The bridge shook constantly, while we stood still. In a little while, the noise of the planes receded, and the bombing ceased. The SS guards returned from their shelter and put us on the move again.

Why didn't they abandon us then and there and leave us to die in the flames and chaos of the destruction? I cannot say. Indeed, this entire march made no sense tactically for them. They were at more risk staying with us and pushing forward. I am convinced now that they did not have a plan. They may have started with a destination in mind, but eventually, our route became a meandering one with no rhyme or reason.

Looking back now so many years later, I have a theory. I believe that we became an excuse for these soldiers to escape from the fighting. They had been ordered to take us away from the camps to conceal the atrocities occurring in them. If this order were abandoned, the next order for them would be directly to the front lines of the war. We were their evasion plan. Unwittingly, they had run right into the thick of the fight.

On this particular day in Dresden, I am quite sure they wanted us to be killed on the bridge. When that did not happen, they decided to keep marching us onward. Perhaps they concluded that the American and British planes knew those of us standing on the bridge were not the enemy and avoided it as a target. Once there was a break in the bombing, they saw an opportunity to get out of the city and away from harm.

We continued our journey toward the southern edge of Dresden. The rubble in the streets made every step an obstacle course. The smoke was so thick it was hard to breathe. The SS pushed us on trying to increase our pace. Just a few minutes after we had all crossed the bridge, more air raid sirens began to blast and, once again, the sound of planes began to roar overhead. More bombs began to drop, and the explosions shattered our ears.

Several bombs landed very close behind us. The force almost shook us to our knees. We looked back and saw that the bridge we had just crossed was gone. A few minutes longer there, and the fate that both the guards and we had hoped for would have come.

HELMBRECHT'S HELL
FEBRUARY 1945

The bombing and firestorm in Dresden had been an emotional roller coaster ride. We had cheered at seeing the bombs fall thinking we would soon be put out of our misery. We had hoped that the air raid might be fatal for our captors as well. Neither hope was fulfilled. The SS guards were still with us and marched us out of the city without anyone having died.

From Dresden we headed southwest. We were becoming weaker and more exhausted. Sickness and disease were increasing rapidly. We were infested with lice, and typhoid and dysentery were prevalent. Many of the women could hardly walk. Afraid that they would be shot for not continuing, they struggled on. Many girls wrapped their arms around those who were struggling and pulled them along. Some of those who could not stand were dragged along the ground by their friends. If they had been left, they would have been shot or left to die in the road.

Yet, our pace did not slow. They drove us onward without mercy. In the first three weeks of the march, we went from Grünberg to Dresden, a journey of about 200 kilometers. We would cover the same distance during the following three weeks. My memory of those weeks is very cloudy because each day was so much like the one before. We marched through village after village of Saxony, each one seemingly exactly like the last.

There is no way I could remember the names of those smaller towns, but I still have some vivid scenes in my mind of some of the places we stopped. Strangely though, I don't remember the road signs, buildings, or landmarks. I remember these mostly because of the food we were given at the end of the day. They stick out based upon what the soup was like, the amount of bread we were given, or whether we got nothing at all.

The weather turned cold and snowy again during this stretch. Once again, nature joined in the cruelty of our captors. I was lucky to have shoes. I can still see the blackened, frostbitten toes of some of the other women. I remember several times seeing girls leave the ranks to grab some snow to quench their thirst. The immediate reaction from the guards was to club them and beat them as they ordered them back into line. Girls died every day and our numbers were dwindling rapidly.

Somewhere around the beginning of March we reached the town of Oelsnitz. I remember this town not because of the food. I remember it because a large group of girls who were very sick were taken away on a truck while we were there. Where they went, I have no idea. I am quite sure they were not taken to a hospital. We never saw them again. I do not know if any of them survived.

After a day in Oelsnitz we were once again on the move. Our next stop would be the absolute worst experience of the march. And it would last an excruciatingly long time. A few days later, we reached the city of Helmsbrecht. They took us to a munitions factory outside the town that also was a concentration camp with female slave laborers, none of whom was Jewish. They were mostly

Slavs from Eastern Europe. There were also a few political prisoners, some French and even some Germans.

When we arrived, we were relieved to see that, even though it was a concentration camp, there was no evidence of furnaces or gas chambers. Our relief would not last long when we got to know our new commandant. We were certainly glad to see Jäschke, the commandant who had been with us on the march, leave us for good. Our new overlord, Alois Dörr, was equally cruel and found ways to torture us for the least "offenses."

Immediately after we arrived, we were stripped completely naked, and our clothes were taken away. They took all our possessions except for our shoes. Long ago, I had sadly lost the box of photos I recovered at our house in Częstochowa. But I had managed to hold on to a small picture that I had of my mother and me. I folded it into fours and tucked it into the toe of my shoe. I still have it today and it is the only picture I have left of any of my family. I knew by now that these cruel beings did not want us to have photos of our loved ones.

One of the other girls managed to keep several photos when they took everything from us. A few days later, she slipped off behind the barracks to have a look at them while one of the non-Jewish prisoners spotted her. The guards were informed, and they quickly came to get her. They shaved her head and forced her to stand out in the cold for 24 hours. Every few hours they doused her with water to make the cold excruciating. How could human beings devolve into such cruel animals? She was not hiding money or gold. She was not hiding jewelry or food. She was not hiding a gun. She only sought to keep these precious pictures of her family!

Somehow, the woman survived this and the march and lived to emigrate to America. Even though I knew the potential punishment for keeping the photo, I was determined not to part with it. I took my chances and fortunately was never discovered.

On our arrival at this new camp we stood naked in the cold, wondering if we would ever get our clothes back. At first, we did not know the reason they had taken them. They made us stand there for hours. Were they trying to freeze us to death? Later in the day, they brought us some other clothes to wear, not our own but some odds and ends of clothing they had stockpiled. We learned that they had taken our clothes to be boiled and fumigated to rid them of lice and other germs. But they did not return these to us. Instead, they brought us these ill-fitting clothes taken from who knows where. The clothes must have also been boiled to sanitize them, because when we got them, they were still wet. We had to put on damp clothes in this freezing weather.

We were divided into two groups and put in different barracks. Some of the women who had become ill were sent to an infirmary. We learned they were not being treated in any way—no medicine, no care for their wounds, and no additional food. They were only separated to keep their sicknesses from spreading.

The barracks we were assigned to had no bunks and no floor. It was dirt with a minimal amount of straw covering it. The barracks had no heating and no toilets or other facilities. At night, the doors of the barracks were bolted tight so we could not leave. At the door of the building were two buckets for us to relieve ourselves. Only two buckets for several hundred women. It is not difficult to imagine the filth and stench that ensued from that situation. And many of the girls had contracted dysentery adding to the problem. On top of that, the guards would come in the morning, see the mess the excrement had created, and begin to beat us in anger and call us every foul name they could think of.

The food at Helmsbrecht was the worst we had in any camp. Some days we did not get any food at all. When we did it was only meager rations. Usually, there was some soup, but it was like drinking dirty dishwater. In fact, I would not be surprised if it wasn't made with that. If we were lucky, it would have a few cabbage leaves floating in it. We didn't get bread every day but when we did, it was such a small piece it did nothing to alleviate our hunger.

Every day, they made us stand for roll call at three different times. They stretched the roll calls out as long as they could to add to our torture. Sometimes they lasted over two hours. We had to stand perfectly still and silent no matter the weather. The timing of these was sporadic and it was different than those of the non-Jewish prisoners. The only good thing about being here is that we were not made to work.

We were glad we did not have to work, but the waiting around in such uncertainty was almost as painful, at least mentally and emotionally. We never knew when the next attempt to break us down further would come. More than a few times they made us stand in the barracks while they dripped freezing cold water on us from the rafters above.

Every morning, women were found having died in their sleep. And every morning they rolled squeaky wheelbarrows in to haul them away. Some days there were so many. Other days, only a few. But every day we lost more girls.

The camp was encircled by high fences with sharp razor and barbed wire stretched thickly across the top. An electrified fence ran parallel just inside the main fences. It always seemed ironic to me that the only prisoners here were weak, sick, and exhausted women yet, they seemed to think they needed a fortress suited for the strongest of men.

We would be here for almost five weeks. Every one of the survivors that I knew said this was the worst part of our ordeal—as one put it, "five weeks of hell." Day after day we were humiliated and dehumanized. We waited to die, and we begged to die. Many of us got that wish.

One day after several weeks there, we heard planes in the distance. We all rushed outside to see them. Their humming grew louder and louder and soon they were directly overhead. They were American planes! Once again, just as in Dresden, we cheered and waited for their bombs to drop. We thought, please, destroy this evil place! Reduce it to rubble. And obliterate us with it! But no bombs dropped. The planes flew quickly out of sight. We were disappointed that our misery had not come to an end, but we knew now that the Allies were getting closer and there would be an ending to this horror story soon.

A few days later, another squadron of Allied planes returned. Once again, we rushed outside to cheer them. To our amazement we did see them begin to drop something as they flew over. But they were clearly not bombs. Above us floated thousands and thousands of leaflets. They dropped to the earth like birds drifting in the wind. We waited for them to reach us, but the guards quickly forced us back inside the barracks and bolted the door before they hit the ground. I think a few of the girls did eventually find some of them. But they could not understand the English they were written in. We did not know what they intended to communicate in this message. But we rejoiced that this sent our captors into panic. In a few days, we would be on the move again. Away from this hell, but what awaited us on the other side?

BACK ON THE MARCH-NEUHAUSEN
FEBRUARY 1945

We knew the American forces were getting very close. And, of course, our captors did as well. The day finally came for us to leave, but this time, it was not just us. The entire camp was evacuating. The Allied soldiers would soon overrun the camp.

The guards brought back the clothes they had taken from us when we first arrived. This seemed strange to me. Why had they kept them from us for so long? Probably in another attempt to humiliate us. What we had worn for the past five weeks did not fit and looked ridiculous on us. Some felt it was a sign that they were beginning to fear what the sight of us in these odd clothes would signal to the Americans if they were overtaken. I don't know, but it was good to have my clothes again even if they were ragged and thread bare. And they were clean again.

We were lined up in the courtyard and roll call was taken. I noticed how much quicker this one had taken than those at the beginning of the march. I did not know how many of us there were left, but it was only a few hundred now—out of 1,000.

When the roll call finished the commandant, Dörr, came out to make an announcement. He told us that the greatest enemy of Adolf Hitler was dead. Franklin D. Roosevelt, the president of the United States, had died. He emphasized that this would be the fate of all of the Führer's enemies. I am sure he included us in that group. The staff of the camp soon joined us in the ranks. The gates were opened and we marched through them in the rain, led by the commandant.

Lili, Halinka, and I tried to comfort one another. We were not much more than an hour away from the camp when a shot rang out behind us. One of the girls could not continue walking and a guard killed her when she fell to the ground. Her body was left in the road and we continued marching. "Stay strong and don't give up," I said to my two friends. "We can survive now that the Americans are so close."

A little while later, two more girls fell behind. An SS guard shouted at them and when they did not respond, he took them into a nearby forest. In a few seconds we heard two shots ring out. A little further down the road, two more prisoners were shot as they collapsed to the ground. Lili, Halinka, and I resolved to help one another to keep up. But Halinka was deteriorating fast and she was struggling more than the two of us. I was worried since she didn't saying anything.

The logic these killlers used to determine who would live and who would die was indeterminable. Of course, logic for madmen cannot be expected. By the time we departed Helmbrechts, the number of sick girls at the "infirmary" there had dwindled significantly as they succumbed to death. We assumed they would be left to die at the camp. But rather than leave them behind to be discovered by the American forces or take them along and slow the march, the commandant arranged for them to be taken by truck to a nearby town. At the same time, he arranged for a wagon pulled by a tractor, to accompany our ranks for those who became sick or too weak to continue the walk. Despite this provision, the guards often simply executed those who could not keep up. It made no sense to us.

The weather continued to get worse on this first day from Helmbrechts. That night we reached the town of Schwarzenbach. We were taken to a fenced yard just on the outskirts of town. The sick prisoners who had been taken from Helmbrechts by truck were already there.

We settled down for the night in the open field. They made no attempt to find us shelter. They gave us no food, not even the sick girls. We were aching with hunger and depleted by exhaustion. The night was getting colder by the minute.

A few hours after we arrived, the guards began to round up the sick women to take them away. What was going to happen to them? We fully expected that they would be shot. I am not sure how many there were of them, but my guess was a few dozen. The women were taken away, some of those too weak to walk were dragged as we watched in horror. To our relief, we learned later that the mayor of the town had arranged for them to sleep in a nearby building and out of the elements.

The next morning we awoke to find many stiff bodies on the ground. The combination of the rain earlier in the day, the lack of food, and the frigid night air made it one of the deadliest nights on the march.

We began our march again without being fed. From Helmbrechts we marched toward the southwest, but now we were moving directly east toward Czechoslovakia. We could see very clearly that we were heading into the mountains. The terrain would soon become steep and rugged. And the cold would intensify.

That evening we arrived in the town of Neuhausen. Along the way, more women who collapsed or could not keep up were senselessly shot. What insanity had taken over these killers? Could they not have fit on the wagon? Once again, we were made to sleep outdoors and had not been given any food since we left Helmbrechts. If this continued, there is no doubt all of us would be dead soon.

We learned after the war that, while at Neuhausen, Dörr had received an order from his superiors in the SS to stop killing and harming those of us on the march. The order alerted him that the Americans were close behind and would soon overtake him. He was told negotiations were taking place for a truce and he should prepare to release us all and allow the Americans to take us into custody. He was also commanded to destroy all documentation related to his concentration camp.

Dörr ignored the order.

ONTO CZECHOSLOVAKIA WITH NO FOOD
MARCH 1945

The insanity of this march cannot be easily explained. The very evil nature of it and the hundreds of murders along the way is enough to condemn it to madness and psychopathy. There seemed to be no rational reason for it either militarily or politically. Why would these trained SS troops force us on a march on which they would be also at risk? Whey would Dörr refuse to follow the order to end it? As we realized how close the Americans were and how badly the war was going for the Germans, my theory seemed ever more plausible. This was their plan to escape being sent to fight on the front, which was ever closer by the hour.

They were not reluctant in the least to kill us. Why did they not just kill us all and be done with it? It would have been the easiest and least problematic solution for them. While they kept themselves fed and generally warm, it was no easy march for them either. It was cold and wet most days. The terrain was mountainous for much of it. And since they chose to take less-traveled routes to avoid interaction with people in population centers, the roads were rough and in bad repair. Had this task ended, what else would they have to do? The Germans were already enlisting children to take up arms at the front. If the march did not continue there is no doubt these soldiers would have been assigned to fight.

Not all the guards liked their odds on the march. It was here in Neuhausen that some of the SS guards had their fill. After Dörr disobeyed the orders to abandon the march, he felt he must leave Neuhausen as soon as possible. Realizing that the Allied forces were very close, he gave the order to continue the march that evening, under cover of darkness. As we prepared to start walking again, chaos ensued. A group of women SS guards took advantage of that and slipped away into the night. Some of the prisoners also took advantage of the confusion and ran into the nearby forest. Testimonies after the war indicated that about 50 of the Jewish prisoners attempted the escape with only seven of them being recaptured.

The rest of us, too sick and weak to attempt running or just too scared to do so, started marching again into the cold dark night. It is impossible to understand how we made it through that night, stumbling blindly along the road, weak and starving. We had not been fed for several days. We had not slept the night before. Eventually the morning light came, and we arrived in a little village called Neuenbrand. From there we hobbled along to the town of Haslau. They let us rest in a farmyard here for a few hours. But they still did not feed us.

The farmer who owned the land petitioned the SS guards to allow him to take some of the weakest prisoners to a nearby factory. Whether they were to be treated and cared for I never found out. Perhaps the guards were glad to be rid of them burdening the progress of the march and they were just left there to die. Either way their hellish journey had ended. I envied them.

After the short rest, we began to march again. We went through a couple of small villages and finally arrived at a farm in the town of

Hoeflas. We spent the night in the barns and sheds at the farm. This was the first night in a long time that we had shelter. Inside these buildings was fodder for the farm animals. Some of the women were so hungry that they ate the fodder. Even with my intense hunger, I could not bring myself to eat any of it. Most of them got very sick afterwards. Later that night, the farmer, along with some of his neighbors, brought us some cooked potatoes to eat. It was the first food we had eaten in several days.

The next morning, we were on the move again toward Bukwa. Along the way, one of the women tried to escape when we came to a stream in a little valley. I suppose she thought she could get across the stream and into the nearby woods. She did get across the stream, but one of the SS guards fired three shots to kill her. This was the first killing of a prisoner since Dörr had been given the order to stop shooting the prisoners. It would not be the last.

We reached Bukwa later in the day and encamped in a meadow there. As I have noted before, I remember most of the places by the food we were given (or not given). Even when it was bad, which was most of the time, it brought relief from the stabbing pain of hunger. Here in Bukwa our captors did something very uncharacteristic and ordered the local baker to give us some bread. They brought us scores of loaves and we devoured them before bedding down for the night.

The next morning, we were on the march again to the town of Zwodau. When we arrived, they took us to a concentration camp. To our surprise, there were some women here who had been left in Grünberg because they were too severely ill to march. Another group of women who had fallen severely ill at Rehuas and were also sent here. They were not receiving any medical attention. Our captors were just holding them here until they died. These women joined us on the march when we left here.

After the war, it was revealed in Dörr's trial that he intended to march all of us from Zwodau to Dachau, the infamous death camp in Bavaria. He changed his mind after he learned the Americans had already taken Dachau. He set his sights on Austria, where he believed a mountain fortress was being built for retreating soldiers and Nazi sympathizers to escape the onslaught of the Allies. When we finally left Zwodau, we started in that direction. But from now on he would become more erratic and impulsive in determining the direction of the march. This would be both a blessing and a curse for those of us condemned to continue walking.

We were not forced to march the day after we arrived in Zwodau. A must-needed rest but very little else. They were still not feeding us. Many girls would die here before we started again. The following day we started out marching to the south toward Austria. Dörr was eager to avoid the Western front where the Americans were progressing. He also wanted to avoid larger towns where he might encounter some resistance. To get to Austria, we would have to march through Czechoslovakia. Dörr was rightly concerned that at this stage of the war, the Czechs might not be very accommodating. As a result, our path along the border of Czechoslovakia and Germany became a twisting and turning one.

We marched that day from Zwodau through Falkenau and onto Lauterbach. At Lauterbach, the mayor had prepared a space for some German soldiers who were in retreat to bed down for the night. When we arrived, the mayor told Dörr that the soldiers had not shown up and that he could use the space to house the prisoners and others on the march. Dörr was delighted, not because he wanted a comfortable place for the prisoners. Instead, he took the hall, which had been filled with straw to make bedding, and put his guards and other staff there. We were sent to a nearby sports field for the night. Once again, we were out in the open and they didn't feed us. To make matters even worse, it became very cold and started to rain. We huddled together through the night to try to keep each warm in the extreme conditions. Moans and groans could be heard all night long. By morning, another dozen women were dead.

The next day, we marched much further. The fact that there were still some of us alive after those past difficult few days astounds me. On this day, we marched through several towns whose names I cannot remember and probably never knew. In every town more of us perished. After the war, witnesses came forth to tell stories of the girls who died in their towns. Sometimes their names could be determined in some way, but in most cases their identities remained unknown. Our captors often left the bodies to rot on the road, not bothering to bury them. Many of the locals in these towns gave them proper burials after Dörr and his henchmen were gone.

In the afternoon, we arrived in a town called Sangerberg and the locals came out to see this evil spectacle. As they gazed on us, some of the women being transported on the wagons beckoned the residents to bring them food. Several of the locals answered their pleas and brought bread. But the women guards who stood nearby chased them away. Another male guard beat some of the women who instigated the cry for food with his rifle butt. Another threatened to shoot them. One of the female guards took the bread and threw it to some nearby chickens rather than give it to us. I struggle to understand how these people became so cruel. What happened in their minds to make them so cold-blooded?

We were not finished marching that day. We left Sangerberg and arrived at Hammerhof where we were given shelter for the night in a barn at a farm. Once again, we were not fed. The next few days were like an experience of déjà vu. Every day, we marched about 10 kilometers, and every day, we came to a new town or village and stayed in barns on a local farm. Sometimes we were fed and sometimes not. A couple of times, the local villagers brought us soup and potatoes during that week. There seemed to be no rational reason why our captors sometimes allowed us to receive food, but went to extreme means to prevent it at other times. In a few days we would witness an astounding scene as some local people defied the SS guards in order to give us food.

A DEFIANT GREETING FROM THE CZECHS
APRIL 1945

It was nearing the end of April 1945 and the weather was getting warmer. Our biggest risk now was starvation rather than exposure. Every night more women perished. Sometimes just a few but sometimes a dozen or more. Not all of them starved to death. There were other causes such as typhoid, typhus, gangrene, but we were so often not fed that starvation was usually the reason.

We left Hammerhof and marched through several other villages and towns for the next few days. I cannot recall many details of these days. Everything seemed to blend together. A couple of days it rained hard, while thunderstorms popped up all around us. That night we slept in barns, but many who were soaked from the rain did not make it through the night. One of the owners of the barn tried to bring us some food, but the SS guards prohibited her from doing so. In the morning, we were fed a mixture of bran and hot water that had been mixed in an animal trough before being dished out to each of us.

The next day was one of the most dangerous days since Dresden. As we marched, some Allied airplanes began to approach. We could hear their engines from quite a distance. They grew louder and it became clear that they would soon be over us. Suddenly, one of them dove toward our column and its machine gun began to fire. Bullets whizzed all around us and pelleted the ground. Several of the girls collapsed and died instantly. Other girls were wounded and somehow survived the attack even though they were not given any medical attention. I do not remember if any of the guards were killed.

The strafing killed two of the horses that pulled the wagons loaded with the guards' supplies and prisoners who were too sick to walk. A few of the girls near the horses ripped into the flesh of the carcasses and ate it. It was a dismal and sickening sight.

A day or two later, we crossed the border into Czechoslovakia. It turned much colder as we moved higher into the mountains. Snow covered the ground all around us. The steep rise in elevation was adding to the difficulty of the march. But the greeting we would receive from the Czech people renewed some hope and faith in humanity.

As we approached the town of Domazlice, the villagers came to watch us march by. We were surprised to see they were dressed in very colorful, festive clothing, typical of this Slavic region. Why they dressed this way we did not know. Perhaps it was a Sunday or a holiday. Whatever the reason, their attire did not seem like everyday clothing. To this day, the image of the beautiful hats, dresses, skirts of the women and the shirts and trousers of the men is stuck powerfully in my mind. Especially after the surprising thing that happened next.

Some of the villagers started to sneer and jeer at the SS guards. Their taunting increased until it became cacophonous. Suddenly, people came out from the shops and houses that lined the road. They brought with them all kinds of food—bread, meat, cheese, milk, potatoes, eggs, and more—and they began to throw them to us.

Many of the girls broke ranks from the column and rushed to get the food. The guards fired warning shots in the air and shouted to get back in file. They ordered the locals to stand back. Most of the girls obeyed fearing that they would be shot. But the townspeople shouted back at the SS soldiers and continued to toss the food to us. The townspeople refused to obey, and the guards shouting did nothing to stop it. Fortunately, they decided not to use their guns to intervene, and we were able to keep and eat the food.

Dörr was now determined to get back across the border out of Czechoslovakia and away from any more hostile receptions. He ordered us to continue to march and to pick up the pace. We moved toward a town called Mraken, still inside the Czech territory. Once again, the villagers came out and gave us food. This time the guards did nothing, but pushed us hard to move out of the town as quickly as possible.

It was an incredible sight. Not just because of the food being thrown by all these colorfully dressed people. But also because of the reaction of the women and girls. We were so starved that we dove for the food. We had not seen so much food at one time in years. There was plenty for every one of us. Yet, some fought over small pieces of bread even though there were whole loaves lying on the ground for the taking.

That day is etched in my memory because of the contrast in human nature displayed. We witnessed the compassion of people who risked their lives to give us food that they probably desperately needed themselves in those dark days. Even today, it warms my heart to think of the kindness the locals showed to us. But I am ashamed when I think of the way we fought over the food. I can still feel the shock and anger that gripped me when food was pulled out of my hands by a fellow prisoner. I'm sure we looked like seagulls or squirrels or some other kind of animal, battling one another over a scrap of food. The Nazis wanted to see this kind of behavior from us to validate their belief that we were sub-human.

Their cruelty drove us mad. No human would be above this behavior after being subjected to the terror and deprivation we had faced, not just for days or months, but for years.

We would pay a price for giving into desperation. There was so much food that we gorged ourselves. Now we were not threatened by the lack of food but by too much of it. After being in such a starved state, eating too much food could kill you quicker than starvation. But it was too difficult to resist. Almost every one of us got sick and some of the women even died.

The next day was one of the longest days of marching. It felt as if we had gone twice as far as in previous days. We left Czechoslovakia and were once again on the German side of the border in Bavaria. That night we spent in an orchard and the cold was excruciating.

Later in the evening, we were brought some soup prepared by the villagers in the nearby town. When it arrived us prisoners rushed to be first in line to be served. Even though we were still suffering from the previous day's gorging, our stomachs ached in hunger. Chaos broke out again as the girls pushed and shoved to get the soup. The guards shouted, pushed, and beat us trying to gain control. But we were so hungry they could not quell the ruckus.

Shots were fired into the air. When he heard the commotion, Dörr arrived at the scene. His anger was visible and audible as he shouted for order. His demands were ignored, and the girls continued to push to get the food. Finally, he ordered the guards to take all the food away. Cries and shouts filled the room as it became clear we would not be fed that night. The food was never brought back. Well into the early morning hours I could hear sobs and moans from the starving and sick girls. Many more would perish during that cold and dark night.

GOODBYE, DEAR HALINKA
APRIL 1945

The next day, after marching through several more towns and villages, we stopped to rest for a little while. The guards allowed some locals to bring us bread and potatoes. Most of us were very sick from gorging. Yet, the hunger pains were still there, only now along with the intestinal pains from overeating. We were plagued with diarrhea and vomiting and constantly excreting one or the other. They did not allow us to stop marching to relieve ourselves. The filth and misery from our soiled clothes were awful.

For most of the march from Helmbrechts, we had at least one wagon traveling alongside to carry prisoners who could no longer walk. But there was not enough room for all of them. Friends banded together and dragged or carried their colleagues to prevent them from being shot, beaten, or left behind to die. Lili and I had to do this for Halinka. She grew weaker by the day, and we worried she would not last long. We draped her arms over our shoulders and somehow mustered the strength to drag her along with us. She could not get on the wagon as it was already overloaded.

After so many more girls got sick from overeating, Dörr realized he should obtain more wagons to keep the march moving more quickly. Now it was the American forces who were gaining on us rather than the Russians. He ordered locals to bring wagons to carry prisoners. Many complied and soon there were several more wagons accompanying us. Halinka finally was able to get a ride instead of being dragged by Lili and me.

The terrain began to get steeper. It had been difficult enough marching on flatter ground. Now, in a much more weakened state, we had to push uphill. In just a few short days, we climbed almost 500 meters in elevation. The weather deteriorated quickly as we ascended. A mixture of snow and rain began to fall, and we were getting soaked again. We shivered uncontrollably.

For days, my feet had been very cold, and now I was losing feeling in them; I knew frostbite was starting. Somehow, I managed to keep putting one foot in front of the other even though it was like walking on pins and needles. With each step the snow got deeper and the road muddier. It was impossible to keep from stepping in the slushy puddles of water. Without relief I knew this would soon be the death of me.

Dörr had mostly ignored the order to stop killing prisoners. The records of Dörr's trial establish that over 50 prisoners were murdered after the order was issued. But now he was reluctant to encourage these killings. However, he did little to prevent them by the SS guards. Several of them did not share his reluctance and were quick to solve the problem of a weakened or escaping prisoner with a pistol.

We were glad that Halinka was now on a wagon and we did not have to worry about her dying at the hands of one of these monsters. Her condition was getting worse with each passing hour. I noticed that her left arm was swelling greatly and looked as if it would explode. Her breathing became shallow, and her eyes were glazing over, her skin was pale and ashen and much of her hair had fallen out. Eventually, she no longer responded to us.

Lili walked alongside the wagon to monitor her. I could not keep up with my aching feet, so I limped along getting further and further away from them. Lili tried to give her some water or bits of food that we had saved, but sadly she could no longer ingest it.

Lili climbed into the wagon and took Halinka into her arms. I watched from behind while the wagon moved forward shaking and shifting in the cold, wet afternoon. The other prisoners on the wagon seemed oblivious to her plight. Like her, they were all close to death.

After a little while, I looked up to see Lili coming back toward me. I knew this was not a good sign. She sidled up next to me and pulled my arm up over her shoulder to support some of my weight and take the pressure off my feet. A tear welled in her eye. She couldn't say anything. She didn't need to. I knew that Halinka was finally at peace.

The wagon did not stop. We did not stop. We kept marching. There was no recognition of our friend's passing. Not from the other prisoners on the wagon. Not from the other prisoners marching, and certainly not from our captors. Only Lili and I mourned her, but even we did so silently.

Halinka's parents had sent her a beautiful royal-blue coat while we were at Bolkenhain. It was her prized possession and had helped her survive the brutal cold. The coat did not have a hood and Halinka did not have anything to cover her head. At Grünberg, Lili and I decided to make her a hood to match her coat. We created a hood from a sweater we found to fit over the collar of the coat. We were lucky to find some blue dye that was very close to the original color of the coat. Halinka was so grateful for it. It kept her from freezing during the long roll calls at Grünberg. Not long after Lili left Halinka to join me again on the march, we noticed another woman wearing Halinka's coat.

I prefer to remember the acts of sacrifice and bravery among our fellow prisoners. There were many and I like to believe there were more of these instances than of those when we turned on one another for survival. I cannot say for certain that was indeed the case. There were times we fought each other for scraps of bread when we were almost starved to death. There were many instances of theft of things that were necessary to stay alive. The Nazis kept us in desperation to dehumanize us and break us down psychologically. At times it worked, and we succumbed. I am disgusted by the thought of Halinka's coat so callously being taken from her, but I do not fault the woman who took it. She was a victim of that cruel tactic. We were sad to see another person wearing it, but we understood the woman's desperation. I'm sure Halinka would have preferred someone use it rather than have it thrown away.

I wondered what would happen to Halinka's body. We hoped that she would get a proper burial, but we were powerless to do anything about it. Death came every day of the march. In just three months, our numbers dwindled from over 1,000 to about 300. At every stop, more women were left dead or dying. Sometimes they were buried, but mostly not. If they were, it was usually in some shallow, unmarked grave, and sometimes in a mass grave dug by fellow prisoners.

Many years after the war I learned that Halinka had initially been buried in one of these shallow graves alongside the road where she died. But some local Czech people had found her body and had her reburied in a memorial cemetery established in the Czech town of Volary where the march officially came to an end. Its mayor had taken it upon himself to create the cemetery for the victims who had died in Volary and in nearby towns. There is a beautiful statue that overlooks the graves. It commemorates the hundreds who died on the march.

ESCAPE AT LAST!
MAY 1945

The day Halinka died was a long day. It was one of the longest stretches of the march. We had crossed the border again, back into Czechoslovakia. We were in the Bohemian Forest, a place renowned for its natural beauty and the idyllic villages and homes that dotted the hillsides. The deep valleys, towering peaks, and dark woods often shrouded by mist and fog gave inspiration for the creation of ghostly tales of evil beasts, monsters, and madmen. Those tales were fiction. But now the storied forest was truly haunted. These Nazis, real-life beasts, monsters, and madmen, spun a tale of terror that none of the old fables could match. Yet, clues that the story might be near the end were starting to appear.

In the last two days, we encountered German soldiers retreating from the war front. Some of them marched alongside us. It was a bizarre scene. Dörr and his guards were increasingly nervous realizing the Americans were drawing closer. We knew it too, but we were so weak we could not think about trying to escape. We simply dragged on hoping that the Americans would overtake us soon.

That evening, we stopped at a farm and were put up in the barns for the night. We were near the town of Prachatice. At these higher elevations the snow and cold intensified. Would they be our final death blow? I do not remember if we were fed that night. Though I was very hungry, all I could think of were my feet. I could no longer feel anything in my toes since they were literally frozen. For days, my toes had been changing color, from pale to green and now to black. Blisters oozed with puss. I realized that gangrene would set in soon, if it hadn't already. Every breath was laborious and I felt as if I was suffocating. I knew that I could not take one more step. I did not sleep much that night. I anxiously waited for the morning hoping to see some sun in which I might warm my feet.

The next day when we were ordered to start marching again, I told Lili that I could not go on. She pleaded with me to find the strength, or else they would probably kill me. I told her I was on the verge of death anyway, so they might as well go ahead. I told her that she must go on without me since she was in much better condition. I resolved to stay behind and suffer whatever fate had in store for me.

Lili thought for a few moments and then said, "I will not leave you. You need someone to help you or you will surely die." She was ready to sacrifice herself for me. We were both certain they would kill us for not continuing on the march. She kept her word despite knowing the risk. I was so thankful for her friendship. She had been the toughest and most resilient of the three of us. Without her risking her life, I would not have survived.

The group of prisoners began to file in and prepare to march once again. Lili and I took our time and carefully moved toward the back of the group. Nearby was the edge of a forest. We agreed that when the time was right, we would make our way there to hide. The prisoners were not marching yet, so we sat down on the grass as close to the woods as we could without being noticed.

Then the order came to begin marching. Lili grabbed my arm and draped it over her shoulder. She lifted us both up as if to join the others. We waited and watched carefully to make sure none of the guards were looking at us. As soon as their eyes were turned, we hobbled into the woods and crouched down behind some shrubs. My heart raced and I gasped for breath.

We watched and listened as the prisoners moved down the road and out of sight. Miraculously, no one had noticed we were gone. At least for the moment. I tried to calm my breathing and relax, but to no avail. We waited for a long time, perhaps a couple of hours or more until we were certain that no one was coming back for us. We had escaped, but now what? We were out in the snow and cold. We had no food. Which would kill us first? Starvation, exposure, or, in my case, frostbite and gangrene? Without help from one of the locals we were doomed.

The Czech people had proved to be compassionate to us before, so we were glad that we were back there rather than in Germany. We were in the country and could not see any houses, but we knew we were near a small village. We went back to the road and started walking in the opposite direction the prisoners had taken. I say "we" were walking, but only Lili walked. She was dragging me along with my arm across her shoulders.

Past a bend in the road, we saw a few houses scattered along the route. Everything was almost completely silent and still. Because I could hardly walk, we decided we would just have to take our chances with the first house we came to. As we approached it, we worked on the story to tell the people who lived there. We decided to say that our houses had been bombed out and that our parents had been killed. We alone had survived and needed help.

When we reached the door, Lili took a deep breath and knocked. After a couple of minutes, the door inched open, and a woman peeked out from behind it. Disbelief covered her face as she looked at our pitiful condition. Her mouth gaped open and she could not speak. It was if she had seen two ghosts back from the dead.

In broken German Lili stammered out our implausible story. I don't remember how, but we had already determined that the woman was German rather than Czechoslovakian. There were many Germans in this region since it was so close to the border. And many had been encouraged to settle there after the war began as part of Hitler's search for Lebensraum, or "living room" for ethnic Germans. If she were one of them, this could be the end for us. She probably would not be favorable to fleeing Jews. There is no doubt she had already discarded our lie about who we were and why we were asking for help. She knew exactly where we had come from.

We waited for some response which probably only took a few seconds, but it seemed like forever. To our surprise and relief, she invited us in and led us to the kitchen. Inside, we saw several young children who peaked out from behind the kitchen door cautiously but curiously. She gave us some bread and some eggs to eat. There was plenty for us take, but we had learned our lesson from overeating before. Even though we were starving, we did our best to eat slowly, just a little bite at a time.

Afterwards, she poured some water from a pitcher into a basin. She handed it to me first and told me to wash up. She led me to a room with a mirror and put the basin down on the dresser in front of it. She gave me a towel and left the room. I scooped the warm water into my hands, and splashed it on my face. I will never forget the sensation when my hands touched my cheeks. All I could feel were bones. I may as well have been touching a skull. In fact, that is what I was doing. I raised my head and gazed into the mirror. It was the first time I had seen my face in weeks. All I saw now was skin and bones.

We have all seen the horrifying photos of the survivors of Auschwitz and other death camps just after they were liberated.

The people who survived were walking skeletons with some flesh attached. That is what I looked like at that moment. There is a word specifically for us, "*Muselmann*," Yiddish for Muslims. It was used because people in this condition eventually became so weak that all they could do was sit slumped over like a Muslim in prayer. How had I managed to keep moving as a *Muselmann*? I still have no answer to that question.

THE GERMAN FARMER
MAY 1945

Good luck shone on us in our first attempt to get help after our escape. We had a little to eat, cleaned up a bit, and rested out the cold and snow for a few hours. Meanwhile, our German host became increasingly nervous. Eventually, she told us that we had to leave. The Americans had not yet captured the area and German troops were still around. She was frightened of being caught helping escaped Jewish prisoners.

We understood and began to prepare to leave. Where would we go now? Could our luck hold out at the next stop? We left the house not knowing the answers to these questions. On the road again we surveyed the area. We knew the road led back to a village that we had passed through earlier. Would it be sensible to go there and hope to find someone who would be compassionate to us? We discussed for a short while. Finally, we decided that it would probably be best to stay away from the more populated areas and off the main road. We had encountered German soldiers while we marched, though we had not seen any for a while. If we did, we knew it would probably not end well.

Mountains rose steeply above the road. We thought we might be safer up there where it was less populated. Perhaps we could find a vacant or isolated house with no neighbors close by. In a remote location such as that we deduced the occupants might not be as fearful to hide us for a few days while we gained strength. We found a footpath that led up a slope, and assumed that a trail would most likely be safer to follow than a road. We started the climb.

The food had given me some energy, so I was able to support myself a bit more. Somehow, Lili continued to keep me upright. I do not know where she found the strength. We struggled up the steep terrain slowly and arduously. I had to stop and rest every few steps, but we kept moving persistently.

After several hours we were high above the main road. A small farm was visible just ahead. We approached it cautiously, stopping every so often to assess the situation. We heard chickens cackling and a cow let out a low, mournful bellow. A column of smoke rose from the chimney. The thought of being next to a warm fire gripped us and we decided to risk asking whoever lived there for help. Once again, we rehearsed the story of losing our homes and families in a bombing raid. At the door, Lili knocked gently. Soon we heard someone shuffling slowly toward the door. The latch lifted and the door creaked open. An old man stood before us. He had a thick beard and deep wrinkles covered his face. He was unkempt and slightly bent over with age. Unlike the woman at the last house, he did not seem shocked at our appearance. But when he greeted us in German, fear raced through my heart.

We told him our invented story and he smiled. From that reaction we knew that he did not believe it either. He stepped back from the door and opened it wider and then beckoned us to come in. He led us to the kitchen, told us to sit at the table and sat down with us. We were hopeful that he had taken us into the kitchen to give us some food. But at first, he offered us none. Instead, he wanted to know more about what happened to us.

After a few minutes of talk he told us he would give us something to eat. But he knew something about hunger and what can happen if you eat too much too quickly. He explained that while he was a prisoner of war in Russia during World War I, he also was on the brink of starvation. He knew what we had learned the hard way, that overeating could mean death to someone in our condition.

So he cautioned us and then gave us some water to drink. I had not noticed how thirsty I had become. Even though there was plenty of water and snow around to partake, I had not been drinking enough. He waited until we finished drinking and then he went to his cupboard and pulled out a few small pieces of dry bread. He gave us each a piece and told us to nibble it slowly. Then he poured some milk into a pan a put it on the stove. After it had warmed, he poured us each a small portion in a cup and told us to drink it slowly. He explained that the water and milk would help fill our stomachs so that we did not feel as hungry.

The man had a kind face and a grandfatherly way about him. His wife had died years ago and only his daughter lived with him. He told us that the daughter suffered from a mental illness, but did not specify what type, and we never saw her while there. His two sons were somewhere fighting in the German army. He had not heard from them in a long time. Even though he didn't express it, we could tell he was worried that he might never see them again. He had no grandchildren, a revelation that made me sad. Memories of my grandfather came rushing back to me and I thought about the joy we had together. After experiencing the kindness from this old farmer, I think he would have been a very good grandfather. I hoped that maybe someday he would become one.

As we sipped and nibbled, he told us stories of fighting the Russians, how he was captured, and of his time in prison. I don't remember them now and I was still so weak that my mind was not focused enough even then to have understood the details. But I realized that those experiences gave him empathy for our plight and condition.

When he had finished his stories and we our food, he laughed and said he knew our orphan story was not true. He figured out that we were Jewish prisoners from the march, but reassured us that he would protect us for as long as he could and help us get back our strength. He looked down at my feet and said we should attend to them immediately. He rose from the table, fetched a basin, and filled it with warm water. He noticed that we were covered in lice, so told us that we would have to stay in the barn; he could not risk being infested.

With the basin of water in hand, he led us to the stable. We were not disappointed, even though we would be roommates with a cow and a pig. The smell was intense, but somehow pleasant because I knew we were finally safe. The barn was relatively warm and there was hay to use for keeping warm. I sat down and put my feet in the water. The feeling in them was still mostly gone so I could not enjoy the comfort of the warmth. The most important thing was getting them cleaned and the blood circulating.

Later, he brought us some blankets. I found a spot in one of the corners and arranged a pallet to lay down on. When I collapsed on it, every bit of my energy evaporated. I quivered as I warmed under the blanket. A great feeling of relief overcame me. For the first time since the war started I felt safe and hopeful that the nightmare might finally end.

THE WAR IS OVER
MAY 1945

I dozed off quickly after lying down in the stable. I don't know how long I slept, but Lili woke me after a while and told me to strip down. She was boiling some water outside the barn to de-louse our clothes. I struggled to pull myself up and slowly disrobed. She had her clothing already off and took mine with her. I grabbed the blanket and fell back down again to the hay. I was beginning to doze off again when Lili returned. She had an annoyed expression on her face. "Are you not going to help?" she asked. I laughed out loud so abruptly that it hurt my sides. "Lili, I can't even stand up," I replied. She was not amused and turned to go outside without a word. I felt bad, but I was so sick that I could not have helped in any way. Our old friend understood that I was too sick to do anything. Somewhat jokingly, he nicknamed me "halb tot" [half dead.]" This was certainly an example of the old saying, "Many a truth is said in jest." He admonished me often to take care of my feet. He checked them every day to see how they looked. Lili understood as well and stopped pressuring me to do the chores.

Those clothes were so ragged and threadbare I thought they might disintegrate in the boiling water. We had nothing else to wear.

The thought of finally having clean clothes regardless of their condition was another welcome relief. Lili worked hard to scrub them as clean as could be, then hung them inside the barn to dry. I pulled the blanket tight around my shoulders and huddled in the corner.

After some time, the farmer brought us a bit more of the bread and milk, warning us again to eat it slowly. We sat down together and nibbled on it. We were so happy for this good fortune. And for a moment, I let my mind wonder about what would be next for us. Of course, this was not a permanent solution. We were certain the war would be over soon if not already, but what would the aftermath be? Nothing was predictable in such chaotic times. Fear and worry began to return.

I forced my mind back to the present. Over these tumultuous years, I had learned not to think too far ahead. All my mental energy needed to stay focused on the immediate future, how to survive the day, the night, or even the next five minutes. For now, we had a bit of respite from the terror we had endured, and we had the hope and promise of a few days to recover. We had some food, we had a warm place to sleep out of the wet and cold. We could clean ourselves. And we felt we could trust this man even though he was a German who had fought for his country years ago. We didn't know him very well and he did not talk about politics with us, but there was something about him that gave us assurance that he would not betray us.

The next few days were quiet and peaceful. I had not experienced this kind of serenity in years. The man continued to bring us food and help us to recover. One afternoon, he came into the barn with a big smile and announced jubilantly that the war was over. The Americans had seized the entire region and were occupying Prachatice, a little town down the mountain from his farm. Lili and I hugged, and tears welled in our eyes. I thanked her for her friendship and told her that without her I would not have survived.

She told me the same was true for me, though we both knew that she had been the stronger one.

With the good news, the reality of this bizarre situation we found ourselves in began to dawn on me. What an unlikely trio of people living on this mountainside farm. Two young Polish-Jewish girls in the mountains of Czechoslovakia living in the stable of an old former German soldier. Before the war, who could have imagined such a scenario. I smiled at the thought of it.

The war was over, but what did that mean? For the short term we were safe, but for the long term, danger and uncertainty still lurked. Looking back now, I know that many Jews died after the fighting ended and the Allies gained control. The end of the war did not save them. They could not overcome the abuse they suffered. I was in danger of that as well. Would the frostbite and gangrene finish what the Nazis had not? I also wondered about the other prisoners with us on the march when we escaped. Did any of them survive or did the guards finally murder them all? I held out hope that the Americans were able to overtake them before that happened.

The next day the German farmer came to check on me again. He could see that my feet were not improving much and he became worried for me. He said that I had to get medical treatment for them soon or it could be deadly. He left immediately to go down to Prachatice. He went to the mayor's office and told them about us and my desperate condition. The mayor found someone to loan the farmer a horse and cart. In a few hours, he was back to load me in it. Lili climbed aboard with us and we headed down the mountain for the town.

At the hospital I was being examined. After a quick look at my feet the doctor told me that he would need to operate right away. There was no time to delay. I was whisked away by the nurses, cleaned up, and taken into the operating room. I had noticed that all the doctors and the nurses, who were mostly nuns, were all German. Now my life was back in the hands of people who had tried so hard to kill me during the war.

These men and women had probably been loyal to Hitler and the Third Reich throughout the war and perhaps longer. Were they Jew-haters like so many other Germans I had encountered? If so, there would be no better cover to kill off one more Jew than during an operation on a patient so close to death. The speed at which they prepared for the operation was evidence that I was at death's door. I had no choice but to trust them since I could not get up and run away. I put the thought out of my mind and then a strange calm came over me.

As the anesthetic began to take effect, I began to feel terribly alone. Lili had returned to the farm with our old German friend, and I wondered if I would ever see her again. In the drowsiness my mind began to flash back through the horrible events I experienced through the war. Halfway between awake and asleep, I wondered if they had just been part of a strange and bizarre nightmare.

HOSPITAL IN PRACHATICE
MAY 1945

I heard voices, speaking softly, comfortingly, but I could not understand them. They were garbled. Hazy light began to fill my eyes. Then I remembered my nightmare. Perhaps once awake from this deep sleep, I would find myself in a bed safely back in my childhood home in Częstochowa. That wishful thought was interrupted by pain in my legs and feet. The light was giving form to a strange bed in a strange room. It was not Częstochowa. It was the hospital in Prachatice. My nightmare was real after all.

I looked down at my feet and remembered why I was here. My legs were bandaged all the way up to my knees. The bandages were not cloth or gauze. They were made of some kind of corrugated paper, like cardboard. The war had so badly disrupted supplies that this hospital had to create makeshift dressings for wounds. What I saw frightened me. They had not told me what they were going to do during the operation, and I had been too afraid to ask. Now I was too afraid to know.

A nurse, clad in a nun's habit, came over to and told me that the operation had been a success and that I was going to be alright. I may have managed a smile, but I was anything but happy. What did that mean? Had they amputated my feet to stop the spread of gangrene? I could not bear to ask, and the nurse offered no more details. Then she reached down and picked me up to carry me to the room where I would begin recovery.

I was taken by surprise. This small woman was able to pick me up with relative ease and carry me down the hall to the hospital bed. I had dwindled down to a literal "bag of bones." I must have felt as fragile as a newborn chick to her. We reached the bed and she lay me down on it, careful not to break me.

My bed was right next to the window of the room and looked out on the street. I could see people going about their day as if nothing had happened over the past six years. The only strange sight were some American military men that occasionally passed the window. I was glad to have this view out into a world returning to normal. But could I ever do so? The world that was normal to me had been destroyed and my family along with it.

I thought of my dear friend Lili. How was she doing? Why did she not stay with me at the hospital? She did not need surgery, but her health was also very bad, and she needed as much care as I did. I knew why she returned with the farmer. Just as she had felt a great responsibility to help me during our plight, she now felt a responsibility to help this farmer with some chores since he had been so gracious and compassionate to us. She went back to help him clean his house and wash some clothes and other tasks around the farm. I respected her for this, but I longed to see her again and hoped that she would come to visit soon.

The next day, the mayor of Prahatice came to visit me. I learned that he had arranged to get me to the hospital at the farmer's request. The mayor was glad to see I was recovering, and that the operation had been successful. He came to the hospital to check on me before the operation. He told the doctors that I was a Jewish survivor and that he would hold them responsible for my fate. He instructed them to do everything they could to bring me back to full health. The fact that he felt compelled to intervene in this way made me realize my worries about the doctors being German was not unfounded. His visit was very comforting to me and, from then on, I was able to trust the hospital staff.

Two days later, the nurses came in to change my bandages. They took me back to the operating room and laid me on the table. I still did not know if they had amputated my feet or not. As they peeled off the layers one by one, my heart began to race. I felt faint and struggled to breathe. I still did not have the courage to ask them if my feet were still there. I kept my head flat on the table and refused to look while the last layer was taken off. The nurses assessed the healing with one another. Then one of them told me to sit up and look. I hesitated. She told me again to look. The inflection in her voice gave me courage. I slowly sat up and looked down.

My feet were still attached!

The tension left my body along with the pressure of the deep breath I had been holding as I sat up to take the look. Not only were my feet still there but all ten of my toes. Not one had needed amputation. I did not develop gangrene. Delaying one more day, perhaps even one more hour, my fate might have been different. I lay back on the bed, closed my eyes, and for the first time in years I felt I was finally out of danger.

The next day I had a great surprise. Lili came to visit me. We hugged and she sat down on the bed to talk. She told me of all the things she was doing for the farmer and that he was grateful and treating her well. When it was time for her to go, I begged her to stay with me. I so desperately wanted her company and I knew she also needed more care than she could get at the farm. She needed some rest rather than working so hard.

My pleading finally convinced her. The nurses allowed her to stay if she shared my bed which was not large, but since we were so tiny there was plenty of space for the two of us. We sat on the bed and looked out the window. Two American soldiers wearing battle helmets and shouldering rifles passed by. We turned and smiled at each other.

NURSING BACK TO HEALTH
JUNE 1945

Several weeks had passed since my operation. I was healing slowly but successfully. I still could not walk, but I was gaining weight. During those weeks, the nuns fed me liberally. They had been so shocked at my weight loss that they were eager to bring me the best food in the hospital. They even brought me food from a storeroom in the basement that was mainly for the doctors. At times, they gave me some wine to drink with my dinner. Not only was it delicious, but it also served another purpose. They believed it would increase my appetite, and they were right.

Every day for those first few weeks, one of the nurses carried me to the scales to weigh me since I could not walk. They stood on the scale with me in their arms because I couldn't stand on my feet. They got very excited at every additional kilogram the scale showed. I was also glad to gain weight, but I was starting to get fat. Looking back now, I am not so appreciative of their zeal to fatten me. I have struggled with my weight since. But after being a *Muselmann*, I am decidedly happier with my current weight problem.

One day, the mayor came back to visit us. He noticed our clothes. They were ragged and torn. Lili had cleaned them up as best she could, but they were not suitable anymore. He said he would help us get some better clothes. He and Lili left immediately to look for them. The clothing stores in the town had not yet re-opened. But nearby was a warehouse containing possessions stolen from Jews by the local Germans. I had no idea how these had been identified and confiscated. In the warehouse were lots of clothes. The mayor took her there to select some for us. She returned with skirts, blouses, trousers, hats and scarves, underwear, and shoes. They were all still in very good condition. What a delight to have decent clothes again! Gradually, we were beginning to feel human again.

Lili and I were enjoying our time together. It was the first time to get to know one another without the threat of death at every moment. We enjoyed watching life in Prachatice outside our window, especially the handsome American soldiers.

One day I awoke and looked outside. It was a beautiful summer day. The morning sun lit up the buildings along the street and everything seemed clean and refreshed. I threw open the window and leaned out to breathe in the warm air. People were moving about briskly as they went about their daily routines. I watched them walking effortlessly and wondered when I would be able to do the same.

In a few minutes, an American soldier passed right in front of me. He said hello and stopped. I was delighted that he wanted to talk, but I could not speak any English, so I was visibly nervous. To my surprise he started speaking in Polish. He did not know the language well, so he stuttered as he spoke. He struggled to put the sentences together and pronounce the words intelligibly, but he knew enough for us to learn a little bit about each other.

He was of Polish descent and had been born in America, so he had not perfected the language. After I told him that I was a Jewish survivor, he told me that some of the American soldiers there were Jewish. He would tell them about me and ask them to come visit me. I was excited about this, but again, I was nervous because I could not speak English. Early the next day, several of them came to see me. To my delight they all spoke Yiddish, so we were able to get to know one another and begin a friendship.

These gallant men were so good to us. They brought us chocolate and other sweets and goodies. They brought us other more practical gifts too, like toothbrushes and toothpaste. Our teeth were in bad shape after years of almost complete neglect, so those kinds of gifts were particularly memorable. The presents they brought were a delight, but the warmth and concern they showed for us was the greatest gift they gave to us.

Our friendship with this group of soldiers grew stronger. Being confined to the hospital limited our chances to get together. I became motivated to work hard to regain the ability to walk. Over the next couple of weeks, I pushed myself to strengthen my legs and practice walking. It was very hard work but eventually I was able to walk again. I remember my first day leaving the hospital on my own two feet. Getting outside was such a thrill. The soldiers came and took us for walks in the evening and we used to go on picnics in the countryside.

By this time, I was almost fully recovered, so we could have left the hospital. Fortunately, the hospital staff did not force us to leave since we did not have any other place to go. I was grateful for this. Had we been in another place where there had been a lot of refugees and survivors, we probably would not have had this luxury. For a long time, Lili and I were the only survivors in Prachatice that I am aware of. At one point, a Hungarian woman came to the hospital to be treated to make a total of three survivors. Had there been many more, I am sure we would have been forced to leave after were healthy enough to do so.

The Hungarian girl was in worse shape than me. It didn't seem possible, but she was even more thin and frail. She was so weak she could barely talk and had a gaping open sore on the back of her neck. I will never forget the sight of it. It was filled with puss and all around it the flesh was rotting away. Throughout the war, I had seen a lot of grotesque afflictions of human bodies, but this one for some reason still haunts me like few others.

RETURNING TO HUMAN
JULY 1945

We were moved by the mayor's concern for us. It gave us reassurance that we would be protected and cared for while in the town. The mayor clearly had not been sympathetic to the German aggression in his country. Others in the area also resented the German occupation and the suffering the war had brought to so many people there and across Europe. We heard stories of attempts in Czechoslovakia to get revenge. Some of the German people had lived there for many years prior to the war since the region was so close to the German border. Some of the Germans living there came after the war started and took land from the Czechs in Hitler's goal of finding "living space" in Eastern Europe for Germans. Hitler had made it clear before the war that Bohemia and Moravia, which this part of Czechoslovakia was part of, had belonged to the German people for thousands of years. During the war, he annexed it and Germans came to claim land they thought was theirs.

Now that the war was over, the Czechs wanted the land back and took steps to seize property. An organized plan was crafted to expel thousands of Germans from the region. Certainly, this plan was justified, but no doubt some of the Czechs took advantage of it to seize property from innocent people. We despised the Germans for what they did to us. We often thought that given the opportunity for revenge, we would kill them all. Despite this, we would soon find ourselves helping to prevent one such land grab.

One day, our German farmer friend showed up at the hospital. He was afraid and distraught. The locals in the area were attempting to seize his property claiming that he was a supporter of the Nazis. He had come to ask for our help. He wanted us to tell these people about the help he gave us to prove to them that he did not hate Jews. We agreed enthusiastically and without any hesitation.

A few days later, there was a hearing for him to defend himself against the accusations and the attempt to seize his farm. Strangely, we were not taken to a court or any type of government building. We were taken to a house in the town and up to an attic room where the German farmer sat in front of several local Czechs. It was a strange atmosphere. The room was tiny with a low ceiling and was very dark. The men ready to question him did not look like judges or officials of any kind, but ordinary citizens. It was not our duty or place to question the validity or legality of the "hearing," but it seemed like some kind of "kangaroo court" to Lili and me.

We told our story, heaping praise upon our friend for his efforts to help us. We were clear to point out that, not only had he risked his own life to help us, but also went to great length to give us care that saved our lives. The tribunal listened carefully asking very few questions. Once we had finished, they thanked us, and we left not knowing what his fate would be. In a few days, we learned that our testimony had been successful. It proved to the locals that the man was not a Nazi, and they did not take his farm from him.

Today, I am often asked about how I feel about the German people. It's a natural and fair question considering the unparalleled evil they wrought upon European Jews. I will say that during those terrible years, I developed a hatred as deep as any possible. I imagined the terrible ways I would pay them back. Many other Jews felt the same. How could we not have these feelings? After the war ended, a few Jews in some areas did take revenge carrying out isolated killing sprees on Germans. But for most of us, it was only a fantasy and one that would soon dissipate. I know that I could not have stomached it. I had seen too much killing already. I never wanted to see another one again, even for such an evil enemy.

However, we were very eager to see justice brought to those criminals and murderers who planned, ordered, and executed the attempt to eradicate an entire race of people. There was great satisfaction in seeing the various trials of the Nazi leaders and their henchmen after the war. But the fact that Lili and I were able to help this man, even though he was German, gave me great satisfaction and helped heal my hatred for those who tormented us so cruelly. It was a lesson learned that returning good for evil is the only way to stop the cycle of hatred. The Germans saw us as animals, lower than animals in reality. They did everything to dehumanize us and make us behave like animals. Sometimes they were successful, for example, when the women prisoners fought each other for food. But in the end, we kept our humanity and rose above it.

I am sad to say that we lost touch with the German farmer soon after the war. We never saw him again after the hearing. The prewar Czechoslovakian government, which was democratic and duly elected, had been reinstalled. But it was coming under great pressure from the communist party and would soon fall under Soviet control. Foreseeing this, our American friends made plans to get us out and into Austria which would remain under US control for a few years after the war. We never have the chance to return to Prachatice to find our friend and thank him. It saddens me that I don't even remember his name.

ON TO AUSTRIA
JULY 1945

The day came for us to leave Prachatice. We had been there for about three months. We were taken to the nearby town of Volary where we were happy to learn the rest of the prisoners who marched with us had been liberated. Once there, we learned about how the march ended for them.

As the Allies closed in on him, Dörr eventually realized he would have to free the women. He was indecisive about when, where, and how. About half of the women could no longer walk and were being transported on wagons and trucks. These were taken to a local furniture factory to be housed while Dörr decided what to do next.

Even though they knew their time was running out, some of the SS guards were not through with their killing. At one point after we left the march was strafed by Allied planes killing and wounding some of the guards. In retaliation, they shot 12 randomly chosen women. The guards were angry that only they had suffered casualties and none of the prisoners had been harmed. So they took out "revenge" upon these innocents.

In another cruel incident, a group of 22 women who had escaped but recaptured were marched up a mountain side. The guards forced them to run up the steep slope. As they ran, the guards began to shoot the slower girls who lagged behind. Before it was over, 17 of the 22 had been killed. The other five were spared only because they had just enough energy to run away and hide.

Dörr knew the Americans would overtake him soon and he did not want to be captured while still holding the women captive. He decided to turn the women over to a local "police force" and then made his getaway.

The guards in this "force" were mostly older men too old to fight in the war. They marched the women to the top of a mountain above Volary. Once there, they were herded into a meadow. A steady rain fell throughout the day and drenched them. The guards never fed them.

Nightfall came quickly and the women sat exhausted, hungry and freezing in the cold and wet. It was a long night, and all the women remained in the meadow until the first light of day began to emerge. Gradually, they began to realize they were completely unguarded. The old men had slipped away during the night afraid the American troops would soon find them. Some of the women left the meadow and hid in the nearby woods, but most of the women could not believe they were free. They sat motionless in the field, expecting the guards to return at any moment. They were too frightened and thought running away still meant getting shot.

On May 6, 1945, the Americans arrived in Volary. The march was finally over, and the women were liberated. The killing had stopped but more women would die. Quite a few who lived to see liberation died from their illnesses soon after. Only a little over 300 out of 2,000 women survived the terrible march.

When the American forces arrived at the furniture factory in Volary, they found about 120 women who were near death on the floor. One of the soldiers said that when he first saw them, he thought they were not young girls, but old men. When he asked some of them their ages and found that they were only teenagers, he was shocked. He had thought they were in their sixties or seventies. The women were taken to the hospital in Volary. Wounded German soldiers were evicted to make room for them. Records show that the women weighed on average between 70 to 90 pounds. They were severely malnourished, covered in lice, and too weak to move. Many had dysentery and sores and ulcers all over the bodies. Their feet were swollen and frostbitten.

Meanwhile, at the mountain meadow, the other half of the survivors were finally convinced it was safe to come down. They descended the mountain into the town of Husinec where the local villagers took them in and began to care for them. A makeshift hospital was set up in a school, and the people brought them food that was easiest to digest.

It was mid- to late-July when I arrived in Volary. I would only be there a few days before we were put on trucks bound for Salzburg, Austria. The American troops were eager to get us out of Czechoslovakia before it came under Soviet control.

In Salzburg we would be taken to a "DP camp," or "Displaced Persons camp." There were many of these all over Europe now. Tens of thousands of surviving Jews from all over Eastern Europe were forced into these facilities. Except for the fact that we were not being killed or starved, these were not much better than the camps we had been kept in under the Nazis. They were crowded, not very clean, and the food was bad. In addition, we were basically prisoners there. We were not allowed to go and come as we pleased. We had to get special passes to venture out. We often sneaked out of the camp because the passes were not available or too difficult to obtain.

Nevertheless, life was getting better for us, and I would soon meet the love of my life and my future husband.

DISPLACED WITH LONEK-SALZBURG
JULY 1945

The truck ride from Volary to Salzburg was bumpy and exhausting, and the scenery as we ascended into the Austrian Alps was breathtaking. The hillsides rose steeply above the mountain roads and were lined with typical Austrian homes clinging to their edges. Their brown-and-white exteriors contrasted with the deep green of the grass-laden terrain they sat on.

The journey was rough, but I was excited and beginning to feel hopeful again. My health was much better, but there were some lingering affects from my body's years of neglect and punishment.

We finally arrived at the DP camp. The Americans controlled Salzburg at this time, and it was the center of their operations in Austria. There were several DP camps there, all of which were under the direction of the UNRRA, or the United Nations Relief and Rehabilitation Administration. Established toward the end of 1943, the organization provided aid to the war-torn areas of Europe. It was a forerunner of the United Nations, which was established later in 1945.

The camp was crowded and very spartan. Previously, it had been a military compound of some sort for the Austrian and German armies. Mostly office buildings and other types of buildings, but some of them had been converted into sleeping quarters for the refugees. The beds were not very comfortable and had no real mattresses or bedding. Only straw stuffed inside sheets and pillow cases. Lili and I were put in a bunk in the middle of a large barrack. Austria had more than its fair share of displaced persons, as many of the other European countries were resisting accepting them. As a result, it wasn't always easy to get passes to leave the camp because the authorities there wanted to limit any potential problems and complaints from the locals about being overrun with refugees.

My friendship with Lili grew ever closer and we talked about what we would do in the future. We both had a deep desire to get married and have children. Could life really return to normal again after all we had been through? We were beginning to believe so.

One day, after a few weeks at the camp, Lili and I were sitting and talking on our bunk beds when we noticed two boys walk into the building. They clearly were new to the camp and looked a bit lost. They were cute and we took notice. They entered shyly and surveyed the whole room. Who were they and what were they looking for?

Then suddenly, the two boys were gazing at us unabashedly. The attraction had been mutual and they began to approach us. My heart jumped as nervousness overcame me. I was delighted that they were taking the initiative to come and talk to us.

They introduced themselves and began to tell us the story of how they got to the camp. Their journey from Poland to Austria had been one of twists, turns, and narrow escapes. For weeks they jumped from train to train not knowing exactly where they were going most of the time. They were determined to get to Austria and away from the Soviet controlled areas that were quickly closing down. Along the way, they escaped the pursuit of Soviet soldiers and dodged other authorities policing the railways. They hopped on and off moving trains and clung precariously to the tops of railway cars. They seemed rugged and adventurous but also determined and resourceful. The latter two traits appealed to me greatly. I had learned to develop them for my survival.

Lili and I hit it off quickly with this duo, and we felt like we were friends at first sight. Rather suddenly, however, they said that they had to go and find a place to stay. They had looked around in our barracks and there wasn't one bed available. My heart sank. I knew there were probably no beds left anywhere in the camp. Impulsively, I blurted out," Why don't you take our top bunk here? Lili and I can sleep together here on the bottom bunk and you two can sleep together up there." I couldn't believe the words that came out of my mouth. I turned to Lili fully expecting her to chastise me for making such a generous offer at her expense. To my delight, she heartily agreed and pressed them to accept. The two looked at one another and smiled. We went from strangers to bunkmates in the matter of minutes. Our impulse would not steer us wrong.

One of them in particular had caught my eye. His name was Lonek. He was also from Poland but from the Southeastern part, near the Ukraine. His story was unique and I was captivated by it. He had been in hiding for nine months in a concealed bunker. Many Jews had been hidden in bunkers, but most of them had been found. What made his story unique was the ingenious design of the bunker that kept it from being discovered. More than that, his story was unique because of who built it and hid him and his family. The man who saved them was an ardent antisemite before the war. In 2020, Lonek's story was published in a book titled, *Save My Children. An Astonishing Tale of Survival and Its Unlikely Hero.*

In the next few days and weeks, the four of us would become very good friends. We found ways to get out of the camp and go sightseeing and exploring the town and countryside. We loved going into Salzburg to enjoy the parks and plazas. It was a city filled with music everywhere and there was a renewed optimism budding after the dark days of war. It was a romantic time for us. We went for picnics in the parks, and we especially enjoyed going to a beautiful castle that stood on a nearby hilltop.

Lonek and I were forming something more than a friendship. Neither of us knew what the future held. We knew only that we could not stay here long. We would have to find a permanent life. But where? I feared that our paths may soon have to part. I would not be wrong.

LEAVING SALZBURG
AUGUST 1945

It was a lovely time in Salzburg. Even though we were living in substandard conditions in the DP camp, the area around the city was delightful and such a contrast to what we had seen for the past six years. Lonek and I continued to explore the region as much as we could with the restrictions on our movement outside the camp. We went back several times to the Hohensalzburg castle, the fortress that guarded the city high on the mountain top.

It was during one visit to that castle that I unexpectedly reunited with one of my cousins who I had no idea had survived the war. His name was Juzek, and he was the son of my mother's brother. Lonek and I had been to visit the castle and were on our way down aboard the cable car that took visitors up the steep hill. He was on his way up and we met at the boarding platform as he came off at the top. It was such a bittersweet surprise. It was so good to know that someone in my family had survived, and a sad reminder that almost all the others had perished.

It would take some months after the war, but I learned that several others had also survived. One of my mother's brothers had survived as well as one of her cousins. My uncle's name was Josef, and the cousin was a girl named Rina. Three of my cousins from my father's side also survived—two women, Helen and Lucy, and one man, Paul.

My uncle Josef moved to Israel after the war, and I went to visit him there some years later. On that visit, I learned that Halinka's mother had miraculously survived. Josef had remarried and, coincidentally, his new wife was friends with her. When I found out I was eager to meet her and tell her Halinka's story. One day on that visit, Halinka's mother came to visit. Just before she arrived, my uncle's wife took me aside and forbade me to say anything about Halinka to her. She was afraid it would be too much strain on her bad heart. At the time, I understood and obeyed. Yet, I still deeply regret not being able to tell her about Halinka's heroics and fight to the end. I think she would have wanted to know every detail.

Lonek and I continued to become closer with each passing day, but each day also intensified the uncertainty in our lives. We were intoxicated with our newfound freedom and the reality of surviving history's greatest crime. We had never experienced such a carefree time and leisure. We were enjoying the time resting, relaxing, and playing. At the same time, we were becoming anxious about our future. We had discussed several options, but we knew there were too many unknowns for us to be thinking about marriage. We had no trade, no education, and no prospects. We had no country, no citizenship, and no money. Where could we go? How would we support ourselves?

Like me, Lonek was feeling the need to get his life settled—away from the DP camp. He soon met a friend from his hometown of Tluste in the Ukraine. It was purely by coincidence that they had wound up in the same camp. His friend had once saved him during an aktion by taking him into his family's bunker. They were very happy to reunite. His friend's name was Wilo, and he had already determined where he would go after his time at the DP camp. Wilo was bound and determined to go to Palestine. But it was illegal for Jews to go to Palestine at this time. Doing so was difficult and dangerous. One could be imprisoned or, worse, killed trying to get there.

Despite that, Wilo soon convinced Lonek to go with him. The plan was to cross the Austrian border high in the Austrian Alps and flee into Italy where they would be smuggled by ship to Palestine. When he told me of his plan, my heart dropped. Of course, I was sad that we would soon be apart but, more importantly, I feared for his life. I knew it was fraught with danger in many different forms. Yet, even with my sad heart, I did not have the strength to dissuade him. What other plan could I offer him?

It would not be long until Lonek and Wilo left for Innsbruck, their first stop on the long journey to Palestine. We said tearful goodbyes and I watched them walk through the gates of the DP camp. I was reminded of watching my father walk away never to see him again. Of course, Lonek and I had only known each other for a short while, so the pain cannot be compared. Still, I was overtaken by sadness thinking that I might not see him again.

The next few days were depressing. The DP camp in Salzburg looked even more spartan and uncomfortable to me without Lonek to take my mind off the conditions there. I knew there were other camps around Austria, and I had heard that many of them were not as crowded and difficult as this one. I set my mind to be transferred to one of them. I learned of one near an idyllic mountain town called Ebensee. Its name was Steinkogel, and I asked to be transferred there. Fortunately, I was granted permission and I wasted no time packing up and leaving. In a few days I would find myself in a camp that was much nicer than the one in Salzburg. The beds had much finer bedding and the food was surprisingly good. Best of all, the refugees were not packed in like sardines.

There was not as much to do in this area of Austria compared to Salzburg. It was near a small town which did not have Salzburg's deep cultural heritage. But it was a beautiful area nestled in a mountain valley with a beautiful lake nearby. I felt rejuvenated and freer here. It would be a time to reflect and plan for the next steps in my life. And it was good to be away from the sights and landmarks that reminded me constantly of Lonek.

REUNITED
SEPTEMBER 1945

I had been gone from Salzburg for a couple of weeks when I got an amazing surprise. One day, while I sat in my bunk, a very familiar figure suddenly stood in front of me. It was Lonek! He said hello to me, and we hugged for a long moment. I couldn't believe my eyes! How did he get here? Why was he here? What about Palestine? So many questions to ask, but I was so flabbergasted that I could not ask them. I could only laugh with joy.

However, my joy quickly turned to concern. He did not look well. And I could tell he was also having a hard time speaking. At first, I thought it might be because of the emotion of seeing me again. But he told me he was ill. After he had arrived in Innsbruck, he began to feel badly. Initially, he thought it was just a cold or maybe a mild flu, but within hours he was struggling to breathe. He and Wilo were to meet up in Innsbruck with a few others who were also bound for Palestine. It became clear to them all that Lonek could not make the journey. He would not only endanger himself, but the others as well. Trying to cross the high Alps on foot in his condition was not an option.

Lonek regretfully abandoned his plan for Palestine. He remained in Innsbruck for a few days to rest and soon decided he would return to Salzburg to be with me again. When he learned that I was no longer there, he found his way to Steinkogel. How he managed to make that long trek while barely able to breathe still confounds me. I like to think I was the motivation. And I think he would agree. No matter, he had made it and we were together again.

Unfortunately, it would not be all the time. After a couple of nights at the camp, Lonek was finding it even more difficult to breathe. His chest ached in pain with every breath, and he could not sleep at night. He still hoped that the illness was just a bad flu, but it was becoming more certain with each passing hour, that he needed medical attention and soon. The camp had two Jewish doctors and he went to see them. They determined that his illness was pleurisy and that his lungs were filled with fluid. If the fluid was not drained soon, he would suffocate.

They rushed him to a nearby hospital in Ebensee. The conditions there were very poor since it was a makeshift hospital. It looked more like one of the work camps I had been in during my ordeal than a hospital. There were bunk beds without proper bedding. Only sacks stuffed with straw. Could this place provide the cure he needed? I was very worried for him, but this was the only option for treatment.

The doctors immediately prepared to drain the fluid from his lungs. I was glad I was not there to see it because it was a very painful procedure. They had no anesthesia to give him. Lonek still cringes when he thinks about the needle that was inserted in his ribs to pump out the fluid. The sound of the fluid as it pumped into a metal bucket is as clear in his mind as it was on that day.

As painful as it was, the operation saved his life. He was soon on his way to recovery, albeit a very slow one. I visited him as often as I could and tried to bring some little gift to cheer him up. I had formed a good relationship with the cooks in the kitchen at Steinkogel. I enjoyed teasing them and they me. I used this to my advantage to beg a few treats like cookies and cakes to take to Lonek. There was usually enough to share with his fellow patients at the hospital as well. So, each time I arrived it was like a little party.

As the days went by, Lonek did not seem to be improving. I continued to visit the hospital. I tried hard to cheer them all up, not just Lonek. So I joked and laughed with them the entire time I was there, while deep inside I was worried. I did not dare show my fear to Lonek. Why was it taking so long for him to recover?

One day, I visited and was surprised that one of the doctors wanted to talk to me alone. He told me that they were also concerned that he was not improving. He needed a certain type of medicine made from calcium which they had been unable to get because supplies were so scarce. If he did not get it soon, he would probably develop tuberculosis. I was floored by the news, yet I became determined to do everything possible to get the medicine for him. "Where can I get it?" I demanded.

They suggested that I might be able to find it at one of the other DP camps. I hurried back to the camp and prepared to go immediately to find the drug. My first instinct was to go back to the camp at Salzburg since I knew the doctors there and they knew me. When I arrived, I met one of our friends, Salci Perecman, a Lithuanian Jew who had a very big and imposing figure. Older than we were, Salci was a rough and tough-looking character. When I explained why I was there, he said, "Let's go into town and see if we can find it at the local pharmacy."

Once there, we asked the pharmacist for the medicine. He told us he did not have any in stock. For some reason, I felt he was not being truthful. So, I pleaded with him, explaining that Lonek's life was in danger if I couldn't get the drugs. The man insisted again that he didn't have the medication. Salci must have also thought he was lying because just then, he stepped up to the counter and pulled himself to full height. He peered into the pharmacist's eyes intensely then said in a stern voice, "We need this medication." The man once again denied that he had it. Then Salci slowly reached into his pocket and pulled out a pocketknife. He raised the knife slightly and then plunged it down hard, sticking it into the wooden countertop. Then he said to the pharmacist, "I'm not sure you understood me. We need this medication now." Nervously the man said, "I understand. I'll get it for you."

He turned quickly, found the bottles containing the drug and prepared the dosage as fast as he could. We took it and thanked the man. As we hurried back to the hospital, I thanked Salci profusely between uncontrollable bits of laughter. I couldn't help but laugh remembering the scene of Salci staring down at the pharmacist.

The medication played a crucial part in getting Lonek back to health. The threat of contracting tuberculosis had been minimized and he would never develop it. He remained in the hospital for many weeks before making a full recovery. But he eventually did. We owe our friend Salci much gratitude for helping us.

TO AMERICA
OCTOBER 1945

Once Lonek had fully recovered, we returned to Salzburg. We had decided to live together there, if only temporarily. We still knew that our future would not be there.

One day, we received a very pleasant surprise. Lonek's sister Tusia arrived in Salzburg. She had come all the way from Krakow. She and Lonek's brother had gone there a few months after the end of the war. Lonek was with them too until he decided to go to Salzburg. He was delighted to see her, and I delighted to meet her. But why had she come? She told us that one of Lonek's friends who traveled with him from Krakow to Salzburg had returned to Krakow. He told Tusia that Lonek was very sick. When she heard this, she set out immediately for Salzburg. She was so relieved to find him fully recovered and in good health.

This was the first time I had met any of his family. Tusia and I liked each other very much from the beginning. From that very first meeting, she made me feel like a part of the family.

Tusia told us that she had connected with a family friend from their hometown. The friend was living in Schwandorf, Germany and had invited her to visit him there. Tusia pressed us to go with her on the visit. It did not take much convincing and soon we set off for Germany.

I stayed in Schwandorf with Lonek and his family for a few months. Soon, however, I grew restless. With my newfound freedom, I was eager to travel about and see more of Europe. In those months after the war, it was easy to do so. Often, one could travel on a train without having to purchase a ticket. At the same time, Lonek's family did not have a lot of room for me, so I was beginning to feel a bit in the way. So I bid them goodbye and promised Lonek that we would see each other again soon.

I did some traveling through the autumn and winter of 1945 and into the early weeks of 1946. After that, I went to live with my uncle who had settled in a little town in Austria named Bad Naheim, just across the border from Germany. While there, I learned about a special program for underage orphans helping them immigrate to America. It was a program designed especially for orphans who had no other family to take care of them. Since I was still under 18, I qualified for this special consideration. I had to go to Frankfurt, Germany to apply, which was not too far from my uncle's home in Austria.

Not long after I arrived in Bad Naheim, I got a letter from Lili asking me to come visit her. She had left Salzburg before I did to go and live with her brother who had moved to a small town near Hanover, Germany. I was very eager to see her again, so I was soon on my way.

It was very good to see her again, but my stay with her would be cut short. Only a few days into the visit, I received a telegram informing me that I had been accepted by the special program for orphans and could go the United States. The telegram instructed me to go as soon as possible to Frankfurt where the process would have to be completed. I would need to get some paperwork together and have a medical examination. There was no time to lose. I was sad to leave her so soon and worried that we might not see each other for a long time. At the same time, I was overjoyed at the news and left immediately for Frankfurt.

After I completed the requirements in Frankfurt, I set my sights on returning to Lonek to give him the news and say our goodbyes. Once again, the joy of knowing I would soon be in America was undermined by sadness at the realization that I might not see him after I left. Hopefully we could have a few days together before that and vow to do everything we could to stay in touch.

In a couple of weeks, I was on a train to Le Havre, the port in France where the ship to America would depart. Lonek came to see me off and we had one last kiss on the boarding platform. It had all happened so quickly I had not had time to really process the full implications of the new life I was about to begin.

At Le Havre, I boarded the SS Marine. For an army boat it was surprisingly nicely provisioned. It was not luxurious but quite comfortable and we ate well. The journey would last about ten days and, except for a couple of days of rough seas during a storm, it was smooth sailing.

I'll never forget the day we sailed into New York Harbor, and I saw the Statue of Liberty for the first time. I was experiencing such conflicting emotions, but mostly great joy. I was anxious and nervous. I could hardly speak any English, other than "Hello," "Yes," "No," "Thank you," "Goodbye," and maybe one or two other words. Who would greet me? Where would I be staying? Would they be kind or strict and severe? I worried about all these things, but after what I had been through, I was confident I could survive it.

BUFFALO AND GERDA
MARCH 1946

Once in New York, I was met by representatives of the American Jewish Committee, who had arranged places for us to stay. We were some of the very first Holocaust survivors to arrive in the United States. Our ship was the second boat of survivors to land. We were taken to a boardinghouse in the Bronx with other survivors who were on the voyage with me. We stayed here until more permanent housing could be found for us.

There were about 20 of us in the house. I slept in a room with two other girls. Both were originally from Poland. And by coincidence, just before they came to America, they both lived in Bad Naheim, Austria like me. Each of them had a brother who came on the trip. I lost touch with them not too long after we arrived, and I have forgotten their names, but we spent all our time together those first few days in New York City.

I don't remember much about the house, but one interesting thing is still very vivid in my memory. There was a piano in the main hallway of the house and while we were there a black man would come to play it often. He made it ring vibrantly with many renditions of jazz songs. It was a wonderful sight and sound and so typical of what I expected to see in New York.

I was nervous about venturing out in the Bronx. I spoke no English, and everything was so different from the life I had known before the war. But being in the world's most famous city was too tempting to keep me inside. We did as much sightseeing as we could. I remember traveling on the subways, which only cost five cents a ride. We saw some of the familiar landmarks in Manhattan. I don't remember them all, but how could I forget the Empire State Building? We did not go to the top but seeing it on the skyline was impressive.

On my tenth day in New York, they told me a home had been found for me. A family in Buffalo, New York had volunteered to take me in. I had no idea where Buffalo was. The next day I was on a train heading north.

At the station in Buffalo, a social worker was waiting to take me to my new home. The family that hosted me was Jewish. Their name was Friedman, and I can still remember their address—15 Huntington Avenue. They had a big house with four bedrooms. They had four children, three girls and a boy. Only one of the girls and the boy were still living there when I arrived. The son owned an appliance store, and the daughter was in college. The two older daughters were married. One lived in Michigan and the other was still in the Buffalo area. So, two of the bedrooms were now empty and I had my own room. What a luxury that felt to me after living in crowded bunks for most of the war.

I was happy for the privacy. Since I could not communicate well with my hosts, it was a relief to be able to be on my own and not feel the pressure to interact. Although what I probably needed most was to begin speaking English more quickly. The parents spoke Yiddish, which I understood but did not speak well. Mealtimes were awkward. They spoke to each other mostly in

English, so I had no idea what they were talking about. They tried to include me at times, but, of course, the attempts did not yield much conversation. For a short time I was given some basic English lessons with a private tutor. I kept my Polish-English dictionary on hand at all times.

Just a few days after I arrived in Buffalo, I received a mysterious phone call. When I came to the phone, I heard a woman's voice speaking German! It was great to be able to communicate fully with someone again. She began to ask me about my story. Her questions revealed that she knew a lot about what had happened to survivors in Europe. She asked what labor camps I had been in and when and where I was liberated. Those questions might not seem unusual today since we know so much about the Holocaust now. But in those first few years after the war, not many Americans, even Jewish Americans, knew many details about the tragic story.

This woman continued to ask me questions until she discovered that I had been on the Volary death march. Then she told me that another woman in Buffalo had also been on that march. When she told me her name, I almost dropped the phone. It was Gerda Weissmann Klein. I knew Gerda very well. We had worked side by side in the Landeshut camp on adjacent weaving machines, but had not spent much time together on the march. She was four or five years older than I. At our young age, that was a significant difference. And, of course, I kept close to Halinka and Lili throughout the ordeal. Regardless, I was overjoyed to find out she was living so close.

The woman gave me her phone number. I called her immediately and we met just a few hours later. We talked for hours shedding many tears throughout the entire conversation. It was therapeutic to talk about the horrible things I experienced. Until then, the language barrier had prevented me from doing that. And, even if I had spoken perfect English, no one I had met so far in Buffalo would have been capable of understanding what I went through.

Having Gerda nearby was a godsend. Our time together helped me heal and adjust to the new life ahead of me.

Gerda had married an American lieutenant that she met in Volary after being liberated. He was from Buffalo, and they settled there. She wrote a book about her experience on the march. It was the first comprehensive account of the Volary march to be written. It won several awards and Gerda became well known. As a result, she became a human rights activist and a speaker about the Holocaust. Her story was made into a short film that won both an Oscar and an Emmy.

Gerda and I became very good friends. After she gave birth to her first daughter, she asked to help her get home from the hospital. She wanted me to carry the baby to the car when it was time for them to leave. I was honored. Trying to be fashionable to show my gratitude, I showed up in very high heels. Gerda took one look at them and said she would not allow me to carry the baby in those shoes. She was afraid I would stumble and drop the baby!

My friend Lili had written to me that she was working hard to find a way to get to America. Gerda was instrumental in helping her. She and my hosts, the Friedmans, worked together to make it happen. Soon she was with us in Buffalo. What a joy to be together again with my dear friend! She had helped me to survive, and I loved her like a sister. Lili met and married her husband in Buffalo and lived there until she died. Even though I eventually moved to the New York area, we remained close friends until her death.

What a whirlwind those first few weeks in America had been for me. Less than a month before, I was skipping about Germany and Austria enjoying my new freedom. Then in two weeks I was on a ship for America. Twenty days later I was in my own room in Buffalo. And in just two more weeks, I would be sitting in an American high school classroom, still not able to speak a word of English.

In September 1946, I entered Bennet High School as a freshman at the age of 17. All my classmates were younger than me by two to three years. In adulthood that is not a significant age difference, but in those early teen years it is huge. I had not been to school in over seven years. Culturally I was very different as well, and that added to my isolation and alienation. I really felt out of place and a bit ashamed. Knowing that I had a good reason for being behind in my studies did not ease my discomfort.

Nonetheless, I was motivated to study hard because of these feelings and became determined to catch up to the older students. I focused on school and studied long hours every day. I petitioned the administrators at the school to allow me to forgo certain classes that were less academic such as physical education and home economics. They agreed and I doubled up on other advanced classes required to graduate.

My efforts paid off, and in two long years, I was ready to graduate. My teachers and classmates were astonished. And so was I! My English was not perfect yet by far, but I was able to understand and communicate very well. The local Buffalo newspaper featured my accomplishment in an article. I was very proud of that and still have the clipping today.

SURVIVING AMERICA
1946-1948

Those two years seemed to go by fast in some ways, but very slowly in others. Especially the first year. I really missed Lonek. We were able to stay in touch by writing letters, but they came too slowly and not often enough. I worried that we might not see each other ever again. If so, would he meet someone else? Lonek was envious that I got to America before him. But he never showed it when we parted. Instead, he used it as motivation to find a way to do the same. We remained patient and encouraged one another in our letters. In the meantime, Lonek's aunt was doing everything she could to get him to the States.

His mother's sister had immigrated to New York years before the war. As she saw antisemitism rising all over Europe, she pleaded with Lonek's family to leave Poland and come to the US. But Lonek's father had built up a successful business over many years and he did not want to lose it. Going to America and starting over was just too daunting for him. He spoke no English and he knew that most immigrants wound up working in sweat shops and remained poor after settling there. He was aware that Hitler was a threat but could not foresee the evil plans he had for Jews. His father spent a lot of time in Vienna while he served in the Austrian army. From that experience, he felt the German people were the most civilized and cultured people in the world. Once it was too late, he was shocked to see them stoop to such barbarianism.

The weeks turned into months, and I wondered if Lonek would ever be able to come to America. Then one day, I received wonderful news in a letter from him. He had obtained a visa and would soon set off for the United States. It had taken him a little over a year after I left, but finally it was a reality. In October 1947, he came on the SS Ernie Pyle, one of the most famous ships that brought Jewish immigrants from Europe after the war.

His family in New York took him in and he began his long road to becoming American. It would be another two months before we could get together. On New Year's Eve of 1948 I met him in New York. We celebrated the new year with much joy. It was good to see his siblings again and meet his extended family for the first time. That New Year's week went by too fast. It seemed I was back at school in Buffalo before I had left. I wondered when we would see each other again. It would be a long five months before that would happen.

The end of the school year in Spring 1948 was near. I was very certain that I was going to have enough credits to graduate high school. So, I invited Lonek to come to Buffalo to help me celebrate. He could not attend my graduation ceremony because of space limitations. However, he did escort me to the prom. He was a very good dancer, and we had a marvelous evening.

We began to plan how to get Lonek to Buffalo. Once again, my wonderful friend Gerda came to the rescue. She and her husband offered to let him live with them for a while. Not only did they take him in, but Gerda's husband found him a job as a shipping clerk in a local sporting goods shop.

While he was in Buffalo, our relationship grew stronger. We decided to get married, but we both knew we needed to be more established before we could make the commitment. How would we make a living? Where would we eventually settle? It had been a blessing to be in Buffalo, and I was very tired of the severe winter weather. The snowstorms that spawn off the lake can bury cars and houses. I was lucky that my hosts were able to get me some winter clothing, especially snow boots, which were very hard to find after the war.

I finished school and thought about going to college. But I felt the pressure to begin to make money. I was tired of being a charity case. I longed to be self-sufficient and have my own place to live. So I decided to find a job rather than apply for college. I was hired as a laboratory assistant in a local dental lab. It was great to finally have some spending money and begin to save a little bit.

The summer passed by quickly and Lonek and I had a lot of fun together. This was the first time we had enjoyed consistent contact for an extended period of time since Austria. But it would end again too soon. After six months in Buffalo, his brother Edek asked him to return to New York. Edek had bought a small grocery store in Brooklyn with a loan from their aunt. He needed help to run it and pressed Lonek to join him in the new venture. He was sad to leave, but realizing this might be the key to our future, he returned. The business struggled and they eventually had to abandon it. Lonek worked at several other jobs following that, all of which he found very unsatisfying. Eventually he and his brother invested in a real estate company that was building houses and apartments. The real estate market was beginning to explode as there was great demand for housing following the war. They got into it at just the right time. The business grew quickly, and it would be his livelihood until he retired.

Lonek and I were married on October 24, 1949. We were blessed with a beautiful and loving family, two daughters and a son. Our family life has been one of great joy but also of great heartache. My oldest daughter, Susan, was born in 1952 and lives near me in New Jersey. She has three daughters, Jamie, Danielle, and Carly. Jamie and Danielle are married now and are starting their own families. Jamie has given us two great-grandchildren, a boy, Liev Max, and a girl, Rafi.

My youngest daughter, Nina, was born in 1967. She has two beautiful children with some very creative names. Her boy is named Xander, and her daughter is named Drew. We don't get to see her as often as we wished since she and her husband, Noah, now live in Los Angeles.

My son David was born a little over a year after Susan and was very bright and intelligent. We loved him greatly and he brought great joy to us. He was doing extremely well as a communications major at Boston University when he was diagnosed with brain cancer. His brave fight against the dreaded disease was inspirational. Sadly, after two years of chemotherapy, surgery and various treatments, he passed away. It was two years of hell and agony for all of us. We miss him greatly, but remember him fondly and lovingly every day.

LOOKING BACK

My story is one of unbelievable luck. So many times during my fight to survive, fate turned in my favor. And even after the horror was over, luck continued to shine on me. I was lucky to be one of the first survivors to be allowed to America. Once there, I was lucky to find myself living near people with whom I had endured the ordeal. They gave me much needed support and an outlet to process what had happened. I was lucky to have met Lonek and his family. They became my family since I had lost almost all of mine.

Many Holocaust survivors could not bear to talk about their experiences for many years. Some never did. Most of them said the pain of reliving the events was too difficult. I was not averse to that pain. But I found that people in the United States who had not experienced the war directly did not want to hear about it. It was too much for them to process. Even Jews whose families came to America before the war and had not lived under the threat, were rarely ready to listen. So we did not find many sympathetic ears, especially in the early years after the war.

Not having an outlet to talk about it would have been difficult for me. So once again, I was lucky to have some friends nearby and a new family with Lonek to share our grief and pain. Whenever we were together, we were never reluctant to talk about it. We did not force our children to listen to our stories of the horror. But we also never shrank back from talking about it if the subject came up in our many get-togethers with family and friends. If the children were in the room, we continued to talk, not hiding anything from them.

You often hear that the trauma we experienced can be passed down through generations. I think my children and grandchildren have a healthy understanding of what we went through; not obsessing over it, but also not ignoring it or trying to run from it. In fact, we made several trips to Europe over the years to revisit my hometown and other places along the death march, taking along our children and grandchildren on those trips. We made several trips to Lonek's hometown of Tluste, now in Western Ukraine, to help them understand his story. And several times as a family we have visited Yad Vashem, the Holocaust remembrance center in Jerusalem.

In 1985, we visited Częstochowa and found the apartment that I grew up in before the war. I was surprised to find it pretty much the same as I remembered it. It was bittersweet to visit. Some happy memories as a very young girl rushed back, but also the pain of losing my mother and father.

In 1995, the town of Volary along with other nearby Czech towns held a commemoration of the 50th year since the end of the war in Europe. Living survivors of the Volary death march were invited as honored guests. It was a very special ceremony.

There is a cemetery in Volary where some of the girls who died near the end of the march are buried. It is quite remarkable. It is believed to be the only memorial in Europe where mass-murdered Holocaust victims were given individual, marked gravestones. A group of American soldiers were responsible for the cemetery. After they liberated us, they searched the surrounding areas for bodies of girls who had died or had been killed. They forced the German citizens in the area to exhume bodies from shallow graves and bring them to the cemetery to be buried properly. Every victim was given a Jewish burial, an individual grave site, and a headstone. In the middle of the cemetery stands a beautiful statue to honor the victims of the march. The bronze statue is over 3 and ½ meters high and is an abstract female form.

At the ceremony we were greeted with music and flowers. The current mayors of the towns organized formal receptions and invited us to sign the town chronicles. In one of the ceremonies we joined Volary's middle-school children to help them plant 95 trees, one for each of the victims in the cemetery. It became a living memorial to them right on their school lawn. The children gave each of us a ceramic piece they had made themselves, and we took delight in signing the children's autograph books. After that, we presented the town with a monetary gift that was used to purchase new musical instruments for the school band.

Before holding a memorial service at the cemetery, the women placed candles and flowers at the base of each stone. Several gravestones were marked "*Neznama*,"

the Czech word for "unknown." The mayor of Volary pledged that the town would always take care of the graves as a duty of honor.

My friend Lili gave a short speech saying, "As we stand here, our hearts are aching for our murdered sisters. We thank the mayor for giving us a chance for closure now that we have finally been able to say goodbye and rest in peace." Then we recited a special prayer known as a Kaddish. We closed the service by chanting *El Maleh Rachamim*, a Jewish prayer for the soul of a person who has died.

That night, at a ceremony in the town's movie theater, the mayor presented each of the survivors with a specially minted commemorative silver coin, a statuette modeled on the sculpture in the cemetery, a certificate, and a red rose. It was a tearful reunion, with tears of joy and sorrow.

On that same trip Lonek and I went to Salzburg to visit the place where we had first met, the military compound that was used for the DP camp. We remembered the joy of finding freedom and beginning our lives together. It was good to visit a place with happier memories than those of the terror we had faced.

The tide of antisemitism is rising again in the world. It is frightening that it continues to exist and that so many people continue to deny the Holocaust. Remembering is important. We can never say too many times or loudly enough "Never Forget."

AFTERWORD

I am often asked what lessons I would like people to learn from my experiences. I think they expect me to say something like, "No matter how difficult your situation, no matter how bleak, and no matter the odds, you must dig deep for the will to survive." I do not deny this philosophy can be crucial in such dire circumstances, but I do not believe that I had more will to survive than others who perished alongside me.

What I experienced and the horror we were put through had never before and has not since occurred in human history. What happened to Jews during the Holocaust was so evil and barbarous that a will to survive gave very little power to overcome it. My story is not a usual one that can translate into the usual morals.

I have to say that my story was one of incredible luck more than any power of will or any other attribute of mine. I was a young, innocent, and naive girl. I knew very little about survival in a normal world on my own—much less in one that had sunk into hate-filled tyranny. We had been targeted from the beginning to be eradicated from the earth. They had all the might, power, and will to do so. And they came very close to doing it. The will of a little girl could never have stood against it.

My survival was a series of lucky occurrences. Countless times it could have been me that was selected for execution rather than a girl next to me. Countless times I could have been caught in the crossfire of one of the many aktionen which I witnessed. Countless times I could have starved to death or succumbed to the cold in the rain, the sleet, and the snow.

I saw many women die who marched with me. Most of them were stronger, smarter, and had just as much or more will to live than I. In essence, you could say that I won the lottery repeatedly until the game finally stopped.

I often think about this. I think about the brave men who fought for the Allies who finally liberated us. Millions of them died in that endeavor. They did not win the lottery. I think about the six million Jews who perished. They did not win the lottery. In all, it is estimated that well over 70 million people died during the war. I am sure that most of them had a powerful will to live.

I am not saying that the will to live is not important. Without it, one is finished. But for me it was only a tiny part of the reason why I am still here. I had help from people along the way, some of whom put their own lives in danger to do so. I am so grateful to them. That was more than luck. Those were people who, despite the consequences, were ready to do what was right. Without that, we are all finished. Without my family, most of whom did not survive, I could not have escaped.

I do not seek any accolades or praise for my story of survival. I finally decided to tell it, so that it can be added to the hundreds of thousands of other stories of survival, hoping that future generations never forget.

Once again, remembering is hard. But is something we must strive to do in order that we not allow this horror to ever happen again.

ACKNOWLEDGMENTS

I must express my gratitude and appreciation to Edwin Stepp for his help in creating this book. Even though he was born in America many years after the war, he possessed sensitivity and understanding of the events that took place during the Holocaust. This is unusual for one that did not experience the trauma firsthand.

PHOTOS

Halina and her mother just before WWII. Halina kept this photo in her shoe throughout the march despite great risk of being caught with it.

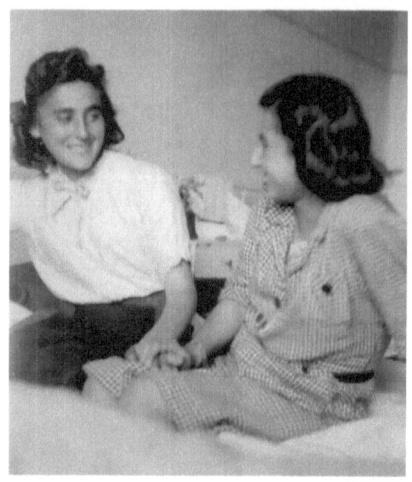

Halina and Lili holding hands on the hospital bed in Prachatice.

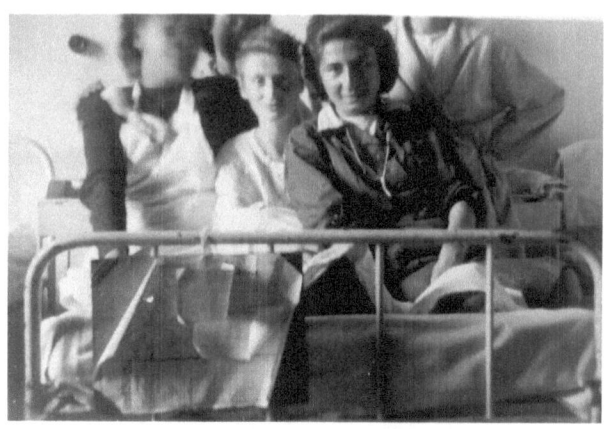

Halina (R) and Lili (L) with the nurses in the Prachatice hospital.

Halina with some newfound friends in Prachatice. She is in the center. Her friend Helen (surname unknown) is lying in her lap and Lili is reclining on the ground just to the right of them.

Halina with another group of newfound friends in Prachatice. Halina is on the bottom left holding an American G.I.'s gun.

Halina posing with two American G.I.'s.

Halina in Prachatice after her recovery in the hospital.

Halina and Lonek say goodbye as she boards the train to taking her to sail away to the United States.

Article in the Buffalo Courier Express in June 1948 praising Halina for finishing four years of high school work in just two years.

Halina visiting the home where her family lived in Czestochowa before the war. It looked much the same as when they were forced out of it.

Graves of the unknown, Volary.

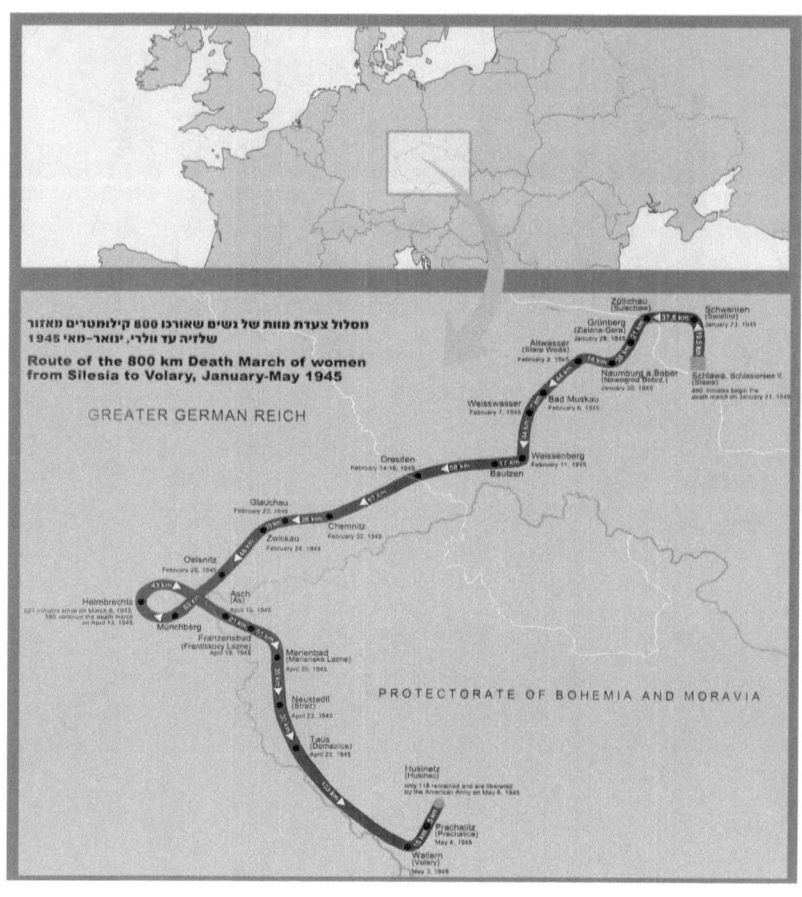

The Volary Death March Route. Copyright Yad Vashem, Jerusalem.

ABOUT THE AUTHORS

Halina Goldberg Kleiner was born in Czestochowa, Poland, in 1929. Her father owned a lumberyard in the city until the Nazis seized it from him after invading Poland in 1939. That began her terrifying story of survival. She was one of the few who survived the infamous Volary Death March. Halina met her husband-to-be, Leon Kleiner, after the war in a Displaced Persons Camp in Salzburg, Austria. They spent most of the next year together getting to know one another and hoping that someday they could marry. Halina was one of the very first Jews to be allowed to immigrate to the United States, and in the summer of 1946, she settled in Buffalo, New York. There she astounded her teachers by completing high school in only two years even though she could not speak a word of English when she arrived. She and Leon reunited in the United States in 1948 after Leon got his chance to immigrate to New York. They married in October of 1949 and started their very successful life together. They had three children who gave them five grandchildren. And now they have two great grandchildren. Sadly, Halina died on April 9, 2022, shortly before her story could be published. She was 93 years old.

Edwin Stepp has more than 30 years experience in media, marketing and advertising. He was executive editor for the quarterly, *Vision—Journal for a New World,* for over 15 years. The magazine had a modest circulation but was distributed in over 75 countries worldwide. He wrote dozens of articles about history, culture, environment and current events for the publication. The magazine had a companion Website that had over 250,000 visitors per month. Edwin lead the development of the Website and also a mobile app for additional distribution of the content. In that position he also helped write and edit several books about Jewish and Christian history published by the journal. In 2011, Edwin founded Django Productions, a television and film production company that focuses on documentaries and nonfiction entertainment. Edwin continues to hone his writing talents as he develops these films and their scripts.

Thank you very much for reading this memoir. We hope you enjoyed reading it and would love to ask you to post a few kind words on Amazon or on Goodreads. Alternatively, if you have read this as Kindle eBook, you could simply leave a rating. That is just one click, indicating how many stars of five you think this book deserves. This will only cost you a split second.

Many thanks in advance!

Halina Kleiner and Edwin Stepp

Should you be interested in the award-winning life story of Leon Kleiner (Halina Kleiner's husband who is called Lonek in this memoir), you can download the Kindle copy on Amazon, or purchase the physical copy in the bookshop, on Amazon, or on Barnes & Noble.

Save my Children by Halina's husband Leon Kleiner is available in English, German and French.

AMSTERDAM PUBLISHERS HOLOCAUST LIBRARY

The series **Holocaust Survivor Memoirs World War II** consists of the following autobiographies of survivors:

Outcry. Holocaust Memoirs, by Manny Steinberg

Hank Brodt Holocaust Memoirs. A Candle and a Promise, by Deborah Donnelly

The Dead Years. Holocaust Memoirs, by Joseph Schupack

Rescued from the Ashes. The Diary of Leokadia Schmidt, Survivor of the Warsaw Ghetto, by Leokadia Schmidt

My Lvov. Holocaust Memoir of a twelve-year-old Girl, by Janina Hescheles

Remembering Ravensbrück. From Holocaust to Healing, by Natalie Hess

Wolf. A Story of Hate, by Zeev Scheinwald with Ella Scheinwald

Save my Children. An Astonishing Tale of Survival and its Unlikely Hero, by Leon Kleiner with Edwin Stepp

Holocaust Memoirs of a Bergen-Belsen Survivor & Classmate of Anne Frank, by Nanette Blitz Konig

Defiant German - Defiant Jew. A Holocaust Memoir from inside the Third Reich, by Walter Leopold with Les Leopold

In a Land of Forest and Darkness. The Holocaust Story of two Jewish Partisans, by Sara Lustigman Omelinski

Holocaust Memories. Annihilation and Survival in Slovakia, by Paul Davidovits

From Auschwitz with Love. The Inspiring Memoir of Two Sisters' Survival, Devotion and Triumph Told by Manci Grunberger Beran & Ruth Grunberger Mermelstein, by Daniel Seymour

Remetz. Resistance Fighter and Survivor of the Warsaw Ghetto, by Jan Yohay Remetz

My March Through Hell. A Young Girl's Terrifying Journey to Survival, by Halina Kleiner with Edwin Stepp

Roman's Journey, by Roman Halter

Beyond Borders. Escaping the Holocaust and Fighting the Nazis. 1938-1948, by Rudi Haymann

The Engineers. A memoir of survival through World War II in Poland and Hungary, by Henry Reiss

Memoirs by Elmar Rivosh, Sculptor (1906-1967). Riga Ghetto and Beyond, by Elmar Rivosh

The series **Holocaust Survivor True Stories** consists of the following biographies:

Among the Reeds. The true story of how a family survived the Holocaust, by Tammy Bottner

A Holocaust Memoir of Love & Resilience. Mama's Survival from Lithuania to America, by Ettie Zilber

Living among the Dead. My Grandmother's Holocaust Survival Story of Love and Strength, by Adena Bernstein Astrowsky

Heart Songs. A Holocaust Memoir, by Barbara Gilford

Shoes of the Shoah. The Tomorrow of Yesterday, by Dorothy Pierce

Hidden in Berlin. A Holocaust Memoir, by Evelyn Joseph Grossman

Separated Together. The Incredible True WWII Story of Soulmates Stranded an Ocean Apart, by Kenneth P. Price, Ph.D.

The Man Across the River. The incredible story of one man's will to survive the Holocaust, by Zvi Wiesenfeld

If Anyone Calls, Tell Them I Died. A Memoir, by Emanuel (Manu) Rosen

The House on Thrömerstrasse. A Story of Rebirth and Renewal in the Wake of the Holocaust, by Ron Vincent

Dancing with my Father. His hidden past. Her quest for truth. How Nazi Vienna shaped a family's identity, by Jo Sorochinsky

The Story Keeper. Weaving the Threads of Time and Memory - A Memoir, by Fred Feldman

Krisia's Silence. The Girl who was not on Schindler's List, by Ronny Hein

Defying Death on the Danube. A Holocaust Survival Story, by Debbie J. Callahan with Henry Stern

A Doorway to Heroism. A decorated German-Jewish Soldier who became an American Hero, by Rabbi W. Jack Romberg

The Shoemaker's Son. The Life of a Holocaust Resister, by Laura Beth Bakst

The Redhead of Auschwitz. A True Story, by Nechama Birnbaum

Land of Many Bridges. My Father's Story, by Bela Ruth Samuel Tenenholtz

Creating Beauty from the Abyss. The Amazing Story of Sam Herciger, Auschwitz Survivor and Artist, by Lesley Ann Richardson

On Sunny Days We Sang. A Holocaust Story of Survival and Resilience, by Jeannette Grunhaus de Gelman

Painful Joy. A Holocaust Family Memoir, by Max J. Friedman

I Give You My Heart. A True Story of Courage and Survival, by Wendy Holden

In the Time of Madmen, by Mark A. Prelas

Monsters and Miracles. Horror, Heroes and the Holocaust, by Ira Wesley Kitmacher

Flower of Vlora. Growing up Jewish in Communist Albania, by Anna Kohen

Aftermath: Coming of Age on Three Continents. A Memoir, by Annette Libeskind Berkovits

Not a real Enemy. The True Story of a Hungarian Jewish Man's Fight for Freedom, by Robert Wolf

Zaidy's War. Four Armies, Three Continents, Two Brothers. One Man's Impossible Story of Endurance, by Martin Bodek

The Glassmaker's Son. Looking for the World my Father left behind in Nazi Germany, by Peter Kupfer

The Apprentice of Buchenwald. The True Story of the Teenage Boy Who Sabotaged Hitler's War Machine, by Oren Schneider

Good for a Single Journey, by Helen Joyce

Burying the Ghosts. She escaped Nazi Germany only to have her life torn apart by the woman she saved from the camps: her mother, by Sonia Case

American Wolf. From Nazi Refugee to American Spy. A True Story, by Audrey Birnbaum

Bipolar Refugee. A Saga of Survival and Resilience, by Peter Wiesner

Before the Beginning and After the End, by Hymie Anisman

Malka Owsiany recounts, by Mark Turkow (editor)

I Will Give Them an Everlasting Name. Jacksonville's Stories of the Holocaust, by Samuel P. Cox

The series **Jewish Children in the Holocaust** consists of the
following autobiographies of Jewish children
hidden during WWII in the Netherlands:

Searching for Home. The Impact of WWII on a Hidden Child, by
Joseph Gosler

See You Tonight and Promise to be a Good Boy! War memories, by
Salo Muller

Sounds from Silence. Reflections of a Child Holocaust Survivor,
Psychiatrist and Teacher, by Robert Krell

Sabine's Odyssey. A Hidden Child and her Dutch Rescuers, by
Agnes Schipper

The Journey of a Hidden Child, by Harry Pila and Robin Black

The series **New Jewish Fiction** consists of the following novels, written by Jewish authors. All novels are set in the time during or after the Holocaust.

The Corset Maker. A Novel, by Annette Libeskind Berkovits

Escaping the Whale. The Holocaust is over. But is it ever over for the next generation? by Ruth Rotkowitz

When the Music Stopped. Willy Rosen's Holocaust, by Casey Hayes

Hands of Gold. One Man's Quest to Find the Silver Lining in Misfortune, by Roni Robbins

The Girl Who Counted Numbers. A Novel, by Roslyn Bernstein

There was a garden in Nuremberg. A Novel, by Navina Michal Clemerson

The Butterfly and the Axe, by Omer Bartov

To Live Another Day. A Novel, Elizabeth Rosenberg

A Worthy Life. Based on a True Story, by Dahlia Moore

The series **Holocaust Heritage** consists of the following memoirs by 2G:

The Cello Still Sings. A Generational Story of the Holocaust and of the Transformative Power of Music, by Janet Horvath

The Fire and the Bonfire. A Journey into Memory, by Ardyn Halter

The Silk Factory: Finding Threads of My Family's True Holocaust Story, by Michael Hickins

Hidden in Plain Sight. A Journey into Memory and Place, by Julie Brill

Winter Light: The Memoir of a Child of Holocaust Survivors, by Grace Feuerverger

The series **Holocaust Books for Young Adults** consists of the following novels, based on true stories:

The Boy behind the Door. How Salomon Kool Escaped the Nazis. Inspired by a True Story, by David Tabatsky

Running for Shelter. A True Story, by Suzette Sheft

The Precious Few. An Inspirational Saga of Courage based on True Stories, by David Twain with Art Twain

The series **WWII Historical Fiction** consists of the following novels, some of which are based on true stories:

Mendelevski's Box. A Heartwarming and Heartbreaking Jewish Survivor's Story, by Roger Swindells

A Quiet Genocide. The Untold Holocaust of Disabled Children in WWII Germany, by Glenn Bryant

The Knife-Edge Path, by Patrick T. Leahy

Brave Face. The Inspiring WWII Memoir of a Dutch/German Child, by I. Caroline Crocker and Meta A. Evenbly

When We Had Wings. The Gripping Story of an Orphan in Janusz Korczak's Orphanage. A Historical Novel, by Tami Shem-Tov

Jacob's Courage. Romance and Survival amidst the Horrors of War, by Charles S. Weinblatt

Join the AP Review Team

Reviews are very important in a world dominated by the social media. Feedback for Holocaust books is more than just a customer review; it also shows the relevance and importance of such books in today's society.

Please go over to the AmsterdamPublishers.com website (top of page) if you want to join the *AP review team*, showing **at least one review on Amazon** for one of our books. You will get updates about new releases and will get the chance to read and review.

www.ingramcontent.com/pod-product-compliance
Lightning Source LLC
LaVergne TN
LVHW091547070526
838199LV00024B/573/J